CORE FOCUS

GRADE 4

TEST PRACTICE
for Common Core

Kelli Dolan, M.Ed., Special Education
Chester School District
Chester, New Jersey

and

Shephali Chokshi-Fox, M.Ed.
Fox Math Consulting

BARRON'S

About the Author

Shephali Chokshi-Fox has been investigating student thinking and problem solving for over two decades. She is fascinated by the complexity and variety of strategies students use in solving rigorous, open-ended story problems. Her role as a K–6 Math Coach allows her the opportunity to understand the interaction between teaching and learning. She provides Professional Development workshops and courses to districts across Massachusetts, has presented at national and regional conferences, and continues to learn about student thinking. Shephali enjoys running, kayaking, and spending time with family and friends, many of whose names are incorporated in this resource.

Kelli Dolan is currently a 3rd-grade teacher at Bragg School in Chester, New Jersey where she has taught for 15 years. She earned a Bachelor of Arts degree in Psychology and a Masters in Special Education degree from Centenary College in Hackettstown, New Jersey. She lives in Flanders, New Jersey with her husband Kevin and their two children, Patrick and Emily.

All inquiries should be addressed to:
Barron's Educational Series, Inc.
250 Wireless Boulevard
Hauppauge, New York 11788
www.barronseduc.com

ISBN: 978-1-4380-0515-7

Library of Congress Control Number: 2014956389

Manufactured by: B11R11
Date of Manufacture: March 2015

PRINTED IN THE UNITED STATES OF AMERICA
9 8 7 6 5 4 3 2

CONTENTS

ENGLISH LANGUAGE ARTS

Reading: Literature

Reading: Informational Text

Writing

Language

MATH

Operations and Algebraic Thinking

Numbers and Operations in Base 10

NOTE TO PARENTS AND EDUCATORS

About Barron's Core Focus Workbooks

Barron's recognizes the urgent need to create products to help students navigate the Common Core State Standards being implemented in schools across America. To meet this need, we have created these grade-specific workbooks that bring the Common Core standards to life and ensure that students are prepared for their assessments. It is our hope that students can work through these books either independently or with the guidance of a parent or teacher.

Barron's Core Focus workbooks are meant to supplement the Common Core teaching that students are receiving in their classrooms. These books, all created by dedicated educators, provide specific practice on the Common Core standards through a variety of exercises and question types, including multiple choice, short answer, and extended response. The questions are organized to build on each other, increasing student understanding from one standard to the next, one step at a time, and they challenge students to apply the standards in different formats. The English Language Arts and Math sections of the books end with a review test—this is a great way to sum up what the student has learned and reviewed from the exercises throughout.

What Is Common Core?

"The standards are designed to be robust and relevant to the real world, reflecting the knowledge and skills that our young people need for success in college and careers."

(2012 Common Core State Standards Initiative)

Simply put, the Common Core is a series of standards that spells out exactly what students are expected to learn in English Language Arts and Mathematics throughout their years in school. These standards are fairly consistent across all grades and are designed so that students, teachers, and parents can understand what students should be learning and achieving at each grade level. Standards are organized in a way that (hopefully) provides a clear understanding of the core concepts and procedures that students should master at each step of the way through school.

Unlike previous standards that were created by individual states, the Common Core is meant to be consistent throughout the country, providing students across the nation with an equal and fair opportunity to learn ELA and Math. They have also been designed to teach students with the intent of helping them apply this knowledge to their everyday lives and experiences.

By sharing the same standards, states can more accurately gauge and compare students' progress and the quality of education received. The ultimate goal of Common Core is to ensure that all students, no matter which state or part of the country they are from, will be equally ready and prepared for college and the workforce.

What Is a Standard?

A standard is a skill that should be learned by a student. Standards are organized by *domains*, which are larger groupings of related standards. For instance, in Grade 4 Math, there are five domains: "Operations and Algebraic Thinking," "Numbers and Operations in Base 10," "Numbers and Operations—Fractions," "Measurement and Data," and "Geometry."

Under the domain "Operations and Algebraic Thinking," there are six standards, which highlight the specific skill or understanding that a student should gain. One standard, **OA.B.4**, directs students to "find all factor pairs for a whole number in the range 1–100"—or learn and know how to find the factors of a number and determine if it is prime or composite.

For example, finding all the factor pairs of 24 are 1 & 24, 2 & 12, 3 & 8, and 4 & 6. Then figuring it is a composite number because it has more than one factor pair.

ENGLISH LANGUAGE ARTS

English Language Arts Standards are separated into different strands. The K-5 standards are comprehensive and are divided into the following areas—Reading, Writing, Speaking and Listening, Foundational Skills, and Language. The Common Core has designated separate Reading Standards for both fiction and nonfiction texts. These standards are identified as Reading: Literature and Reading: Informational Text. Most importantly, the Reading standards attempt to engage all students in the reading process. To meet the standards, students are expected to read multiple forms of text types, and in turn provide deeper literary experiences for all students. The Common Core also emphasizes the importance of text complexity. "Through extensive reading of stories, dramas, poems, and myths from diverse cultures and different time periods, students gain literary and cultural knowledge as well as familiarity with various text structures and elements." (2012 Common Core State Standards Initiative)

Each of the K-5 strands is arranged within a College and Career Readiness Anchor Standard. The Anchor Standards are the overarching goals of a K–12 curriculum. These standards remain constant in all grades. Each grade level's strands are built as a scaffold in order to achieve "official" College and Career Readiness Anchor Standards by the end of the twelfth grade. The College and Career Readiness Anchor standards for Reading: Literature and Reading: Informational Text focus on identifying key ideas and details, craft and structure, and the integration of knowledge and ideas. To meet the Common Core Reading Standards, students are expected to read, respond, and interact with an array of text types of varying complexities. The College and Career Readiness Anchor Standards for Writing focus on text types and purposes, production and distribution of writing, and research to build and present knowledge. To meet the Common Core Writing Standards, students are expected to write persuasive, narrative, and informational text. The College and Career Readiness Anchor Standards for Speaking and Listening focus on comprehension, collaboration, and presentation of knowledge and ideas. The speaking and listening standards heavily focus on students' ability to actively participate, engage, and present academic information in multiple settings. The College and Career Readiness Anchor Standards for Language focus on the conventions of standard English, vocabulary acquisition, and knowledge of language.

The Common Core standards are also designed to help students create digital literature and use technology to communicate ideas and knowledge. The ELA standards are a vision of what it means to be literate in the twenty-first century. These standards foster imperative learning experiences for the twenty-first century learner. "The skills and knowledge captured in the ELA/literacy standards are designed to prepare students for life outside the classroom. They include critical-thinking skills and the ability to closely and attentively read texts in a way that will help them understand and enjoy complex works of literature." (2012 Common Core Initiative)

MATH

The Common Core Mathematics Standards were developed as a connected progression of learning throughout grades K–12. Ideally, this will allow teachers to close achievement gaps and give students the foundational skills necessary to continue their learning. The Common Core provides teachers with an opportunity to build a deep and rich understanding of mathematical concepts. Instruction of Common Core Mathematics Standards encompasses the Mathematical Practices as well. These practices include skills that math students in every grade are expected to master. The Mathematical Practices bring rigor and rich learning opportunities to the classroom.

In grade 4, students develop fluency with multi-digit multiplication and use place value understanding to divide. Students also extend their understanding of fractions to fractional equivalence and decimals. In grades 2, students begin to understand fractions as equal shares and parts to a whole, which is located in the geometry domain for these grades. There is a shift in grade 3, where students are now expected to understand fractions as numbers, such as ¼ and understanding that this means 1 out of 4 equal parts. The Common Core Standards are related across grade levels as well as across the domains. For example, Measurement and Data standards share relationships between Operations and Algebraic Thinking standards. This connectedness helps students prepare for the real world when we do not just use one skill to balance our checkbook or determine the amount of paint needed for a room in our home. We have to be able to apply a variety of skills, and the Common Core Math standards help prepare students for this. The Common Core also supports mathematical understanding of concepts that are developmentally appropriate for students. These standards allow students to build strong number sense in the early grades as they learn to count, order numbers, and compare numbers to help them think about numbers flexibly and understand the relationships between numbers as they move into the older grades.

HOW TO USE THIS BOOK

This test practice workbook is organized by standard—one step at a time—in the order that students will likely see the concepts in the classroom or other learning environment. Each standard is organized in an easy-to-navigate spread(s) providing exposure to the Common Core in the simplest way possible.

Using this book, students will be able to build skills in multiple formats by answering multiple-choice, short-answer, and extended-response questions. Answers and explanations are included at the end of each section so students, parents, and teachers can easily assess the student's response. These explanations are a really important part of the learning process, as they provide information on the understanding needed to answer each question, common misconceptions students have, and an explanation of how a student might best approach the question. Students using Barron's Core Focus workbooks will practice each of the specific content standards as they learn them, and also have the opportunity to review all of the concepts in Math or English Language Arts through the cumulative sample tests.

In addition to the practice spreads covering specific standards, each section ends with a comprehensive practice test allowing students to monitor their general progress in either English Language Arts or Math. Answers and explanations provide additional guidance and instruction.

> A complete listing of all the English Language Arts and Math Common Core Standards can be found at the end of this book in appendices A and B.

FEATURES AND BENEFITS

Barron's Core Focus workbooks provide educators, parents, and students with an opportunity to enhance their knowledge and practice grade-level expectations within the Common Core English Language Arts and Math standards. Each workbook in this series provides questions that specifically correlate to each standard. Every answer explanation provides helpful insight into a student's understanding, identifying common misconceptions and then providing multiple strategies. The books also provide a cumulative assessment for each content area in Math and English Language Arts. Throughout the books, there are helpful boxes that contain a variety of information and expose students to vocabulary, tips, and strategies.

- Parents can use this book to encourage learning at home. This book can be used as guided practice or extra exposure to concepts students may be struggling to master in school.

- Educators can use this book in their classrooms to identify how to assess each standard. Teachers will find that this book gives them insight into what students should be able to do independently in order to master the standard. The detailed answer explanations in the book provide opportunities for teachers to recognize misconceptions students may have regarding specific standards and how to successfully approach questions applicable to each standard.

- Students can use this book at home to build their knowledge of Math and English Language Arts content. They can practice the content they have learned, are learning, or are going to learn. This book can be used to prepare students for what's to come and/or as remedial information for concepts that are posing a particular challenge. The explanations in the book are extremely valuable to students as they work independently, increasing their awareness of concepts and improving their confidence as they work through each question.

The benefits that **Barron's Core Focus** workbooks will provide students, parents, and teachers are endless as the Common Core is implemented in schools across America.

Common Core State Standards Initiative
http://www.corestandards.org/

PARCC
http://www.parcconline.org/

Smarter Balance Assessment Consortium
www.smarterbalanced.org

ENGLISH LANGUAGE ARTS

The English Language Arts Standards are separated into different strands. The K–5 standards are comprehensive and divided into the following areas: Reading, Writing, Speaking and Listening, Foundational Skills, and Language. The Common Core has designated separate Reading Standards for both fiction and nonfiction texts. These standards are identified as Reading: Literature and Reading: Informational Text. In this section, students will practice covering a variety of standards. Each section presents a specific standard covered in Grade 4 and provides the student with practice through multiple-choice, short-answer, matching, and extended-response questions.

UNDERSTANDING TEXT

RL.4.1 Refer to details and examples in a text when explaining what the text says explicitly and when drawing inferences from the text.

Directions: Read each short passage below. Answer the inference questions that follow. Include examples from the text to support your answer.

1. For years Bob had worked at the horse stable near his farm. He loved grooming, feeding, and exercising the horses. He had dreamed of owning his own horse someday. His favorite horse was a brown roan named "Jewel." Jewel was going to foal any day now. Bob was saving every penny he could to try to buy Jewel's foal. His birthday was two days away, and he hoped he would get money for a gift from his parents and grandparents.

   > An inference is when we combine evidence with what we know to come to a conclusion. "Reading between the lines" is a common phrase connected to inference.

   On Wednesday after school Bob rushed to the stable. Standing on wobbly legs was a newborn pony. It was beautiful! The pony had brown and white spots and huge brown eyes. Bob hated to leave the pony but he had to rush home for his birthday celebration. After supper, Bob's mother brought in his cake. He quickly blew out his candles and made a wish. Then Bob opened his gift from his parents. It was money and a bridle!

   What can you infer will happen next? What were the clues in the text that cause you to feel this way?

   _____

   _____

   _____

   _____

2. Kate had recently opened her own restaurant. Her restaurant served various
    types of pasta. Her specialties were lasagna and cannelloni. At first business
    was very slow at Kate's restaurant despite her advertising efforts. Kate decided to
    use a customer satisfaction survey. After several weeks, Kate looked at the surveys.
    Customers seemed very satisfied with the quality of the food, but a number of
    people commented that the prices were steep for the size of the food servings.
    After reading the surveys, Kate decided to create some new advertisements for the
    radio and the newspaper.

    Part A. What can you infer about the new advertisements and the changes Kate will make
    in her restaurant?

    _____

    _____

    _____

    _____

    Part B. What were the clues in the text that cause you to feel this way?

    _____

    _____

    _____

    _____

3. Mary and Beth were excited about Saturday. They had planned a picnic in the park.
    They would ride their bicycles to the park, play for a while, go fishing, and eat the
    lunches they brought. They were also looking forward to walking around the lake and
    feeding the ducks at the park. On Saturday morning, Mary hopped out of bed and looked
    out her window. Her shoulders slumped, and she frowned.

    Part A. What do you know is happening in the text? What clues do you have?

    _____

    _____

    _____

    Part B. What can you infer? Use text-based evidence to support your inference.

    _____

    _____

(Answers are on page 83)

SUMMARIZING TEXT

RL.4.2 Determine a theme of a story, drama, or poem from details in the text; summarize the text.

Directions: Read the poem "The Land of Counterpane" below and answer the questions that follow.

The Land of Counterpane

When I was sick and lay-a-bed,
I had two pillows at my head,
And all my toys beside me lay
To keep me happy all the day.

And sometimes for an hour or so
I watched my leaden soldiers go,
With different uniforms and drills,
Among the bed-clothes, through the hills.

And sometimes send my ships in fleets
All up and down among the sheets;
Or brought my trees and houses out,
And planted cities all about.

I was the giant great and still
That sits upon the pillow-hill,
And sees before him, dale and plain
The pleasant Land of counterpane

1. The setting of this poem takes place
   Ⓐ in the bathtub.
   Ⓑ in a bed.
   Ⓒ in the backyard.
   Ⓓ in school.

2. Who did the boy compare himself to?

_____

3. What is a counterpane?

_____

What clues helped you figure that out?

_____

_____

4. What were some of the things that the boy played with?

_____

_____

_____

_____

5. Did he enjoy staying in bed? Use clues from the poem to support your answer.

_____

_____

_____

_____

6. Do you think this poem happened today or in the past? What clues helped you to decide?

_____

_____

_____

_____

(Answers are on page 83)

DETERMINING THE MEANING OF WORDS AND PHRASES

RL.4.4 Determine the meaning of the words and phrases as they are used in a text, including those that allude to significant characters found in mythology.

Directions: Read the following excerpt from the Greek myth, "The Apples of Idun," paying close attention to the **bold** vocabulary words, and answer the questions that follow.

The Apples of Idun
by Abbie Farwell Brown (1881–1927)

Once upon a time Odin, Loki, and Hœner started on a journey. They had often travelled together before on all sorts of **errands**, for they had a great many things to look after, and more than once they had fallen into trouble through the **prying**, meddlesome, malicious spirit of Loki, who was never so happy as when he was doing wrong. When the gods went on a journey they travelled fast and hard, for they were strong, active spirits who loved nothing so much as hard work, hard blows, storm, **peril**, and struggle. There were no roads through the country over which they made their way, only high mountains to be climbed by rocky paths, deep valleys into which the sun hardly looked during half the year, and **swift-rushing** streams, cold as ice, and **treacherous** to the surest foot and the strongest arm. Not a bird flew through the air, not an animal **sprang** through the trees. It was as still as a desert. The gods walked on and on, getting more tired and hungry at every step. The sun was sinking low over the steep, pine-crested mountains, and the travelers had neither breakfasted nor dined. Even Odin was beginning to feel the **pangs** of hunger, like the most ordinary mortal, when suddenly, entering a little valley, the **famished** gods came upon a **herd** of cattle. It was the work of a minute to kill a great ox and to have the **carcass** swinging in a huge pot over a roaring fire.

Part 1

Think of a **synonym** you would use to replace each word below?
Go back to the passage to make sure the word would make sense when
rereading it.

1. errands   _____

2. prying   _____

3. peril   _____

4. swift-rushing   _____

5. treacherous   _____

6. sprang   _____

7. pangs   _____

8. famished   _____

9. herd   _____

10. carcass   _____

Part 2

Now it's your turn to rewrite part of the myth using the synonyms you just
listed above.

> Even Odin was beginning to feel the **pangs** of hunger, like the most
> ordinary mortal, when suddenly, entering a little valley, the **famished** gods
> came upon a **herd** of cattle. It was the work of a minute to kill a great ox
> and to have the **carcass** swinging in a huge pot over a roaring fire.

_____

_____

_____

_____

_____

(Answers are on page 83)

UNDERSTANDING TEXT

RI.4.1 Refer to details and examples in a text when explaining what the text says explicitly and when drawing inferences from the text.

Directions: Read the following passage and answer the questions that follow.

A Proud Lady in the Harbor

Who wears a crown with seven huge spikes, has an index finger longer than the height of a very tall basketball player, and wears a size 879 in women's shoes? The answer, of course, is the world famous Statue of Liberty. It was the first site that immigrants saw when they arrived in America.

In 1884 France gave the Statue to the United States as a symbol of the friendship these two countries had made during the American Revolution. The huge copper structure was shipped to the United States in 1885 in 214 cases. Over the years, the monument has also come to symbolize freedom under America's free form of government.

The Statue, whose proper name is "Liberty Enlightening the World," stands proudly 115 feet above New York Harbor. It is a tremendous sculpture of a lady, who is dressed in a loose robe. She holds a torch in her right hand, which is raised high in the air. Her left arm holds a tablet containing the date of the Declaration of Independence: July 4th, 1776. People hardly notice the broken shackles underfoot, which represent Liberty destroying the chains of slavery. The seven spikes in her crown stand for either the seven seas or the seven continents.

Millions of people visit the Statue annually. Many visitors climb 354 steps to reach the crown, which contains 25 windows. The normal waiting time to climb to the crown in the summer is three hours. Some visitors take an elevator to the base of the statue, where there is an observation balcony and view of the city. The original torch, which was replaced when the structure was restored in the 1980s, is now at the base.

Today, next to the flag of the United States, the Statue is America's most common symbol for freedom.

1. What is the main idea of this article?
    Ⓐ   The Statue of Liberty has come to symbolize freedom.
    Ⓑ   The Statue of Liberty stands 115 feet above New York Harbor.
    Ⓒ   Visitors climb 354 steps to reach her crown.
    Ⓓ   Lady Liberty wears a size 879 women's shoe.

2. The article states that "millions of people visit the Statue of Liberty **annually**."
    What does the word *annually* mean?
    Ⓐ   daily
    Ⓑ   never
    Ⓒ   yearly
    Ⓓ   weekly

3. Which of the following statements is an OPINION about the Statue of Liberty?
    Ⓐ   The Statue of Liberty holds a torch in her right hand.
    Ⓑ   It was very generous of France to give the Statue of Liberty to the United States.
    Ⓒ   The Statue of Liberty's index finger is longer than the height of a very tall basketball player.
    Ⓓ   Some visitors take an elevator to the base of the statue where they can get a good look at New York City.

4. Why are there broken shackles at the base of the Statue of Liberty? Please answer in complete sentences and refer back to the text.

    _____

    _____

    _____

    _____

5. The article states, "The original torch, which was repaired when the structure was **restored** in the 1980s, is now at the base." A synonym for the word *restored* is
    Ⓐ   damaged.
    Ⓑ   repaired.
    Ⓒ   weakened.
    Ⓓ   ruined.

(Answers are on page 84)

EXPLAINING TEXT

RI.4.3 Explain events, procedures, ideas, or concepts in a historical, scientific, or technical text, including what happened and why, based on specific information in the text.

Directions: Read the following short excerpts from *The Moon* by Seymour Simon and answer the questions that follow.

1. *The astronauts discovered that the moon is a silent, strange place. The moon has no air. Air carries sound. With no air, the moon is completely silent. Even when the astronauts broke rocks or used the rockets on their spaceship, sound could not be heard.*

   The sky on the moon is always black. On Earth, we can see stars only at night. On the moon, stars shine all the time.

   The moon does not have air, water, clouds, rain, or snow. It does not have weather. But the surface of the moon does warm up and cool off. The ground around it gets very hot or very cold because there is no air to spread the heat.

   Using examples from the text and prior knowledge of Earth and the moon, how are the moon and Earth different?

   _____

   _____

   _____

   _____

2. *A footprint on the moon marks the first time that human beings have walked on ground that was not Earth. The footprint may last for a million years or longer.*

   Why will the first footprint on the moon remain there for many, many years?

   _____

   _____

   _____

   _____

3. *Earth and its moon are close in space, but very different from each other. Earth is a blue, cloud-covered planet filled with living things. The moon is a dead world. Without air or water, a cloud can never appear in its black sky and a raindrop will never fall.*

Write a short diary entry as if you were an astronaut who had just stepped foot on the moon.

_____

_____

_____

_____

_____

_____

_____

_____

_____

_____

_____

_____

_____

_____

_____

_____

_____

_____

_____

_____

_____

_____

(Answers are on page 84)

DETERMINING THE MEANING OF WORDS AND PHRASES

Directions: Read the following excerpts from *Dear America: A Journey to the New World (The Diary of Remember Patience Whipple)* by Kathryn Lasky. Based on what you read, determine the definition of the **bold** words.

1. *'Tis hard to imagine what this New World shall be like. I am used to towns with buildings and winding streets. And people **bustling** to market and talking Dutch, or English if they be one of us.*

   Explain in a complete sentence what the word *bustling* means.

   _____

   _____

2. *The **gales** have pushed us back twenty miles! We are practically back to where we were yesterday. I am most depressed.*

   Explain in a complete sentence what the word *gales* means.

   _____

   _____

3. *If it does not work, our ship will founder and sink. I try to imagine drowning in the **snarling** sea. If indeed it comes to that, if the ship goes down, I would hope I would be drowned before a shark would eat me.*

   Explain in a complete sentence what the word *snarling* means.

   _____

   _____

4. *Hummy's mother died shortly before the voyage began so we cannot ask her—and her father, poor soul, is so **melancholy** of his wife's death that we dare not say anything to remind him of her.*

Explain in a complete sentence what the word *melancholy* means.

_____

_____

5. *The sailing master but a few hours before, when he was still set on heading south, brought Mayflower **perilously** close to some dangerous shoal water. The tides ripped fiercely across the shallows and the current against us.*

Explain in a complete sentence what the word *perilously* means.

_____

_____

6. *We plan to go gather many of these clams and mussels for all of us be **ravenous** for some fresh food. There are many varieties of clams.*

Explain in a complete sentence what the word *ravenous* means.

_____

_____

7. *They continued on through groves of walnut trees fairly dripping with nut and then came upon another heap of sand. They **commenced** digging this mound and what should they find but a great basket of most wonderful corn of all colors—some yellow, some red, and some blue.*

Explain in a complete sentence what the word *commenced* means.

_____

_____

(Answers are on page 84)

THE TOPIC SENTENCE AND SUPPORTING DETAILS

> **W.4.1** Write opinion pieces of topics or texts, supporting a point of view with reasons and information.
>
> **W.4.1.B** Provide reasons that are supported by facts and details.

Topic Sentence

Directions: Read the four supporting sentences in each question. Write a topic sentence that goes with those sentences.

1. Topic Sentence: _____

   Supporting Sentences:

   1. Giant Huntsman spiders have leg spans of 12 inches!

   2. The largest species of a tarantula is the Goliath Birdeater.

   3. The "Hobo" Spider builds a funnel shaped web on or near the ground, usually near stones and other low-lying debris.

   4. The Water Spider is the only completely aquatic spider in the world.

2. Topic Sentence: _____

   Supporting Sentences:

   1. There are 50 states in the United States.

   2. Forty-eight of the states form the contiguous United States.

   3. The U.S. borders on Canada to the north, and Mexico and the Gulf of Mexico to the south.

   4. To the northwest of Canada is the state of Alaska.

3. Topic Sentence: _____

   Supporting Sentences:

   1. Whole grains can be found in wild rice and whole wheat bread.

   2. Vegetables can be dark or light in color and offer essential daily vitamins and minerals.

   3. Fruits can be fresh like apples and bananas or dried like raisins and prunes.

   4. Dairy, meats, fish, dry beans, eggs, and nuts also provide daily nutrients that your body benefits from.

Supporting Sentences

Directions: Read the topic sentence for each opinion paragraph starter below. Then add four supporting details that relate to and support each one.

1. Topic Sentence: Students in public schools should wear uniforms.

   Supporting Sentences:

   1. _____

   2. _____

   3. _____

   4. _____

2. Topic Sentence: In order to keep kids healthy, schools should ban junk food.

   Supporting Sentences:

   1. _____

   2. _____

   3. _____

   4. _____

3. Topic Sentence: Dogs are awesome! They make the best pets!

   Supporting Sentences:

   1. _____

   2. _____

   3. _____

   4. _____

(Answers are on page 84)

PRODUCING CLEAR AND COHERENT WRITING

W.4.4 Produce clear and coherent writing in which the development and organization are appropriate to task, purpose, and audience.

Directions: Read the passage below and answer the short constructed-response question that follows.

The Challenge

Mrs. Bertram loved her son, but she worried about him. He was always losing things, and he did not take care of his toys or clothes. She wanted him to be more careful. She wanted him to be responsible.

She was reading a book one morning, or at least she was trying to. It was not easy to do so because Robert was in the hall playing with his drum. Suddenly the drumming stopped and Robert rushed into the room crying.

"I broke it! I broke it," he sobbed. "Your drum?" asked his mother. "How did you do that?"

"I was beating it with the knives and—"

"With the knives!" exclaimed his mother. "Where were your drumsticks?"

"I—I—don't know," sobbed Robert.

"Have you lost them?" said Mrs. Bertram. She needed no words to know the answer. Robert's manner was quite enough. "You know, Robert, what I said would happen the next time you lost anything."

"Yes," said Robert, "You said I must give away all my toys to some little boys who would know how to take care of them."

"Yes," said his mother. "I see you remember. I will send them all to the children's hospital tonight."

"But, mama," said Robert, "if I don't have any toys to take care of, how can I learn to take care of them?"

Mrs. Bertram had to turn away so that Robert would not see her smile. "I will have to think of some other way to teach you to be careful. I will think of something, and I will tell you what to do tonight."

That night, she told him, "I have decided that there is another way you can show how careful you are. I want you to do the laundry every week for two months."

Robert looked astonished. "Boys don't wash clothes," he said.

"Sometimes," said his mother, smilingly. "Now if you do this every day for two months, I will know you have become more responsible. Being careful is part of growing up. It means you are responsible, and it means people can trust you. This is a challenge. It is something to do that is not easy. It will help everyone in the family."

The next week Robert began his work. At first, he disliked it very much. But after a while he changed his mind. He wanted to show his mother he was responsible. He not only washed the clothes, but he also folded them neatly. He kept his toys in a box where he could find them. He was careful with everything.

The day when his two months would be up was Christmas Day. Imagine Robert's delight when he saw he had a new coat, a video game and a new drum and drumsticks. On them was a note: "For Robert, who is very responsible." He felt proud.

Robert learns a very important lesson in this story. What is the lesson he learns? Use evidence from the text to support your answer.

_____

_____

_____

_____

_____

_____

_____

_____

_____

_____

_____

_____

_____

_____

_____

_____

_____

_____

_____

_____

_____

(Answer is on page 85)

PRODUCING CLEAR AND COHERENT WRITING

W.4.4 Produce clear and coherent writing in which the development and organization are appropriate to task, purpose, and audience.

Directions: Read the passage below and answer the short constructed-response question that follows.

The Working Tools of Insects

Insects are wonderful. You need to look closely to learn about them. If you watch them, you will learn a lot.

I wonder if you know that the smallest insects you see about you all have tools that were given to them with which they do their work. There is a little fly called a sawfly, because it has a saw to work with. It is really a much nicer saw than you could make, if you were ever so bold.

The fly uses her saw to make safe places where she can lay her eggs. What is even stranger is that the fly has a sort of homemade glue that fastens the eggs where they are laid.

Some insects have cutting instruments that work just as your scissors do. The poppy-bee is one of them, whose work is wonderful. This bee has a boring tool, too. Its nest is usually made in old wood. This borer cleans out the nest to make it ready for use.

When all is ready, the insect cuts out pieces of leaves to line the nest and to make the cells. These linings are cut out in the shape of the nest. You would be surprised to see the care taken to have every piece of leaf cut so that it is just the right size, so that it will fit just perfectly. When the leaves are fitted, the pieces are nicely fastened together and put into the nest.

Other animals have tools, too. For example, birds have bills or beaks. They use them to get food. A woodpecker uses its bill to drill into trees and get food. Woodpeckers eat insects, so insects need tools to help them escape. Some fly, some crawl. They're all part of nature.

How does the author feel about insects?

Use evidence from the text to support your answer.

How do you feel about insects? What makes you feel this way?

_____

_____

_____

_____

_____

_____

_____

_____

_____

_____

_____

_____

_____

_____

_____

_____

_____

_____

_____

_____

_____

_____

_____

_____

(Answer is on page 85)

DESCRIBING POETRY

W.4.9.A Apply grade 4 reading standards to literature. Describe in depth a character, setting, or event in a story, drama, drawing on specific details in the text.

Directions: Read the following poem and answer the questions that follow.

Wind Song
Anonymous

Here comes the wind, with a noise and a whirr,

Out on the streets he is making a stir.

Now he sends flying a fine, stiff hat,

Tosses and leaves it all muddy and flat.

Turns an umbrella quite inside out,

Tears up stray papers and scatters about,

Makes big balloons out of ladies' long capes,

Skirts into sails, then the queerest of shapes.

The wind is an enemy, often we say:

"We never quite like it—a windy day!"

The wind blows the seeds from their close little pods

And scatters them far away—rods upon rods;

He plants them where never an eye could see

Place for their growing and blooming to be.

He blows away rain, and scatters the dew,

He sweeps the earth clean and makes it all new.

He blows away sickness and brings good health

He comes over laden with beauty and wealth.

Oh, the wind is a friend! Let us always say:

"We love it! We love it!—a windy day!"

1. The second line reads: "Out on the streets he is making a stir."
Who is he?

_____

2. What is author's purpose for writing this poem?
   - (A) to persuade the reader to avoid the wind
   - (B) to teach the reader about the good and bad qualities of wind
   - (C) to warn us about the dangers of umbrellas

3. How does the wind bring good health? Use an example from the text.

_____

_____

_____

_____

4. The author states, "the wind is a friend." This is an example of personification, when a nonliving thing is given living qualities. What does the author mean by this?

_____

_____

_____

_____

5. Is wind your friend or your enemy? Use details from the text to support your answer.

_____

_____

_____

_____

_____

_____

(Answers are on page 85)

DESCRIBING A STORY

W.4.9.A Apply grade 4 reading standards to literature. Describe in depth a character, setting, or event in a story, drama, drawing on specific details in the text.

Directions: Read the following excerpts from *Bunnicula* by Deborah and James Howe and answer the questions that follow.

I shall never forget the first time I laid these now tired eyes on our visitor. I had been left home by the family with the **admonition** to take care of the house until they returned. That's something they say to me when they go out: "Take care of the house, Harold. You're the watchdog." I think it's their way of making up for not taking me with them. As if I *wanted* to go anyway. You can't lie down at the movies and still see the screen. And people think you're being impolite if you fall asleep and start to snore, or scratch yourself in public. No thank you. I'd rather be stretched out on my favorite rug in front of a nice, whistling radiator.

1. Use the context clues to help you figure out the meaning of the **bold** word.

    "I had been left home by the family with the **admonition** to take care of the house until they returned."

    The word *admonition* means _____.

2. Who is the narrator of the story?

    _____

3. What clues helped you figure out who the narrator is?

    _____

    _____

    _____

    _____

But I digress; I was talking about that first night. Well, it was cold, the rain was **pelting** the windows, the wind was howling and it felt pretty good to be indoors. I was lying on the rug with my head on my paws just staring **absently** at the front door. My friend Chester was curled up on the brown velvet armchair, which years ago he'd **staked** out as his own. I saw that once again he'd covered the whole seat with his cat hair, and I chuckled to myself, picturing the scene tomorrow.

4. Name a synonym for the word *pelting*. _____

5. Name a synonym for the word *staked*. _____

6. If you are looking *absently* at something, how are you looking at it?

   _____

7. What animal is Chester? _____

8. Describe the mood the authors created. Why do you feel this way?

   _____

   _____

   _____

   _____

9. How do you think Harold feels about Chester?

   _____

   _____

   _____

   _____

   _____

   _____

(Answers are on page 85)

DESCRIBING A TALE

W.4.9.A Apply grade 4 reading standards to literature. Describe in depth a character, setting, or event in a story, drama, drawing on specific details in the text.

Directions: Read the following tale and answer the questions that follow.

Old Joe and the Carpenter
An American Tale

Old Joe lived in the country. His lifelong neighbor was his best friend. Their children were grown and their wives were gone; they had only each other and their farms. One day, they had a serious disagreement over a stray calf. It was found on a neighbor's land and both of them claimed it. The two men were stubborn and would not give in. They went back to their farms and stayed there. Weeks went by without a word between them. Old Joe was feeling poorly when he heard a knock at his front door. At first, he thought it was his neighbor. When he opened the door, he was surprised to see a stranger. The man introduced himself as a "carpenter." He carried a tool-box and had kind eyes. He explained that he was looking for work. Old Joe said he had a job or two for the carpenter. He showed the man his neighbor's house. There was a new creek running between the two pieces of property, freshly dug by Old Joe's neighbor, to separate their property. Old Joe asked the carpenter to build a fence on his property so that he would not have to look at the creek. He helped the carpenter get started and then went to get more supplies for the fence. The carpenter worked without rest and finished the job all by himself. When Old Joe returned and saw what the carpenter had built, he was speechless. The carpenter hadn't built a fence; he had built a bridge. The bridge reached from one side of the creek to the other. Old Joe's neighbor crossed the bridge; he was quick to apologize for their misunderstanding. He told Old Joe that he could have the calf. They shook hands and thanked the carpenter for his work. Both of them suggested he stay and complete other jobs they had for him. The carpenter declined the work and said he had to leave; he had more bridges to build.

1. What is the main purpose of the story?
   - (A) to teach a lesson about friendship
   - (B) to describe the work done on a farm
   - (C) to tell what life in the country is like
   - (D) to encourage kindness to older people

2. "The two men were **stubborn** and would not give in." Which word is a synonym for *stubborn*?
   - (A) lazy
   - (B) determined
   - (C) shy
   - (D) worried

3. Theme is the message an author is trying to share with the reader. What is the theme of "Old Joe and the Carpenter"?
   - (A) Face your fears head on.
   - (B) Work as a team, and you'll get things done.
   - (C) Honesty is the best policy.
   - (D) Friendship is very important, even when you don't realize it.

4. Why wasn't Old Joe upset when the carpenter built a bridge and not the fence that Old Joe requested?

   _____

   _____

   _____

   _____

5. In the last sentence, the carpenter said to Old Joe that he had to leave since he had more bridges to build. What do you think he meant by that?

   _____

   _____

   _____

   _____

(Answers are on page 85)

DESCRIBING MOOD AND SETTING

> **W.4.9.A** Apply grade 4 reading standards to literature. Describe in depth a character, setting, or event in a story, drama, drawing on specific details in the text.

Directions: Read the following excerpt from *Island of the Blue Dolphins* by Scott O'Dell and answer the questions that follow.

I remember the day that I decided I would never live in the village again.

It was a morning of thick fog and the sound of far off waves breaking on the shore. I had never noticed before how silent the village was. Fog crept in and out of the empty huts. It made shapes as it drifted and they reminded me of all the people who were dead and those who were gone. The noise of the surf seemed to be their voices speaking.

1. What is the setting? _____

_____

How do you know this?

_____

_____

_____

_____

2. Describe the mood the narrator created.

_____

_____

_____

3. List the phrases that create this mood.

_____

_____

_____

_____

4. How would you feel if you were in this setting?

_____

_____

_____

_____

_____

5. Reread the last sentence of the passage and visualize the scene it created. What emotions did that part of the passage create for you?

_____

_____

_____

_____

_____

_____

_____

_____

_____

(Answers are on page 85)

DESCRIBING INFORMATIONAL TEXT

W.4.9.B Apply grade 4 reading standards to informational texts. Explain how an author uses reasons and evidence to support particular points in the text.

Directions: Read the excerpt from *Milton Hershey* by Charnan Simon and answer the questions that follow.

One man who knew all about trying and failing was Milton Snavely Hershey. He tried to set up his own business many times. Each time he failed miserably. He lost all of his own money and the money of his friends and family. But Milton was stubborn. He knew he had a good idea, and he was determined to make it work.

Today, we can all be grateful for Milton Hershey's stubbornness. His good idea was the Hershey Chocolate Company. Thanks to Milton's hard work and determination, we have Hershey's candy bars, chocolate syrup, cocoa, and other treats to sweeten up our world.

Milton Hershey made a lot of money from his chocolate company. He wanted to use this money in a worthwhile way. Instead of spending it all on himself, he used his money to help other people.

Milton Hershey built an entire town called Hershey, Pennsylvania. In this town he built homes, schools, and churches. He also built theaters, swimming pools, a sports arena, and an amusement park.

Perhaps more importantly, Milton Hershey started a school for disadvantaged children. Milton knew what it was like to be young and penniless. He had no children of his own, but that didn't stop him from wanting to help other children. He gave his entire personal fortune to the school that is named after him. Today, the Milton Hershey School serves more than one thousand boys and girls.

1. What word best describes Milton Hershey? Explain why you chose this word.

_____

_____

_____

_____

2. How would you describe how Milton Hershey felt about children? Explain your answer.

_____

_____

_____

_____

_____

3. Do you think the Hershey Chocolate company will continue to be successful in years to come? Why do you feel this way?

_____

_____

_____

_____

4. The overall message of this passage seems to be "if at first you don't succeed, try and try again." What does this message mean to you?

_____

_____

_____

_____

_____

(Answers are on page 86)

GRAMMAR AND THE USE OF PRONOUNS AND RELATIVE ADVERBS

> **L.4.1.A** Use relative pronouns (*who, whose, whom, which, that*) and relative adverbs (*where, when, why*).

Part 1

Directions: Read each sentence below. Underline the relative clause in each sentence and circle the relative pronoun that introduces the clause. The first one has been done for you.

> A relative pronoun introduces a dependent clause that gives more information about a word, phrase, or idea in an independent clause.

1. The gift (that) I got from my grandma needs to be exchanged.

2. My grandfather, whom I respect very much, was in World War II.

3. The grocery store no longer sells the cereal that I like.

4. The woman whose family moved away was very sad.

5. The young girl who lives down the street needs a babysitter.

6. We walked past the church in which I was married.

7. Butterflies, which have beautiful wings, enjoy the warm weather.

8. Last winter we traveled to Paris, which is in France.

9. The bus that I ride to school broke down on the side of the road.

10. My son, who is ten years old, just entered fifth grade.

11. What did you buy with the money that you received for Christmas?

12. Mrs. Thompson, who received the Teacher of the Year award, teaches in my school!

13. Your responses to the survey, which I received yesterday, were appreciated.

14. The little girl who is wearing the purple dress is my daughter.

15. The careless driver who raced through the red light received a ticket.

16. The car that was leased needed to be returned to the dealership.

Part 2

Directions: Complete each relative clause with *why*, *where*, or *when* (relative adverbs).

1. Do you have any idea _____ she is crying?

2. The night _____ you came over I was feeling ill.

3. The school _____ I go to is right up the street.

4. That is the cabinet _____ I keep the pots and pans.

5. I have no idea _____ we are leaving for the airport.

6. I wish she told me _____ she was so upset with me.

7. The police station is _____ you can go if you need help.

8. I remember the year _____ you won the karate tournament.

9. Sections of the town _____ flooding was severe caused people to relocate.

10. No one was in the department store _____ the fire alarm went off.

11. Follow the directions on the map to find out _____ the treasure is located.

12. I didn't know _____ the baby was constantly crying.

13. This is the store _____ I bought all of my school supplies.

14. Mom took me to the restaurant _____ my parents first met.

15. My favorite month is December, _____ we celebrate my birthday!!!

16. Do you know _____ Charlotte is not in school today?

17. I can't recall a time _____ we didn't spend the holidays together.

18. Can someone please tell me _____ the library is?

19. Johnny didn't know _____ he got a low score on his science project.

20. Samantha and Danielle were wondering _____ they would have a sleepover at Sam's house.

(Answers are on page 86)

USING PROGRESSIVE VERB TENSES

L.4.1.B Form and use the progressive (e.g., *I was walking, I am walking, I will be walking*) verb tenses.

Examples of progressive verb tenses:

Present (happening now):
Mrs. Kelly *is giving* us a spelling test today.

Past (happened already):
She *was doing* my homework last night.

Future (will happen):
My friend *will be moving* in the fall.

Progressive verb tenses inform the reader of when an action is taking place. This includes the present, past, and future. For example: *I am walking* (present), *I was walking* (past), *I will be walking* (future). The progressive form shows if the action has happened, is happening, or will be happening.

Directions: Using a complete sentence, answer the following questions using progressive verbs. Pay close attention to the question that is being asked.

1. What were you and your friend doing yesterday after school?

_____

_____

_____

_____

_____

2. What will you be doing with your family this coming weekend?

_____

_____

_____

_____

_____

3. What did you eat for breakfast yesterday?

_____

_____

_____

_____

4. What are you currently learning in math?

_____

_____

_____

_____

_____

5. What would you like to be when you grow up?

_____

_____

_____

_____

_____

6. Describe the first vacation you took with your family.

_____

_____

_____

_____

_____

(Answers are on page 86)

USING MODAL AUXILIARIES

> **L.4.1.C** Use modal auxiliaries (e.g., *can*, *may*, *must*) to convey various conditions.

Directions: We use the modal auxiliary verbs *can, may,* and *must* in the English language for various meanings (ability, possibility, probability, certainty, permission, prohibition, obligation, opinion, speculation, and so on).

Circle the more natural sounding option.

1. The boy looks pretty sick. I think he _____ go to a doctor.

   can   should

2. Grandma has been driving all day. She _____ be exhausted!

   must   should

3. "Mom, you _____ smoke so much. It's bad for your health."

   can't   shouldn't

4. The boy told the cashier, "Hi, I'm lost. _____ you help me?"

   Should   Can

5. You have such a beautiful voice. You _____ sing for us!

   can   should

6. I know she speaks five languages, but _____ she speak French?

   should   can

7. That brand new car looks very expensive. It _____ have cost a fortune!

   must   should

8. Dad yelled, "I _____ believe that you failed your test!"

      can't   shouldn't

9. "I'm on my way. I _____ be there in about 10 minutes," shouted Sally.

      can   should

10. Even though I want that new bike, I _____ afford it.

      shouldn't   can't

11. "_____ I please have another piece of cake, Mom?" asked Johnny.

      May   Must

12. Dad scolded, "You really _____ yell at your sister like that!"

      shouldn't   can't

13. You _____ talk loudly in the library.

      can't   shouldn't

14. She didn't feel well yesterday. She _____ be participating in soccer practice.

      can't   shouldn't

15. Call her now. She _____ be home.

      may   must

(Answers are on page 87)

ORDERING ADJECTIVES

L.4.1.D Order adjectives within sentences according to conventional patterns (e.g., a small red bag *rather than* a red small bag).

Adjectives are words that describe nouns. Sometimes sentences can have several adjectives that describe the main noun in the sentence. When using two different adjectives, the **opinion** adjective always comes first then **number**, **size**, **shape**, and **color** will follow.

Example: I have a big black dog *rather than* I have a black big dog.

Directions: Read the sentences below. If the sentence is correct, write CORRECT on the line. If it is incorrect, rewrite the sentence correctly.

1. The boy has a nice red, oversized sweater.

   _____

2. Mom just bought a giant pink ice cream cake.

   _____

3. They own a silver, short-handled steak knife.

   _____

4. She has a yellow, round dining room table.

   _____

5. She spotted the big shiny diamond in the jewelry store.

   _____

6. Who's that silly skinny man over there?

_____

7. The recipe calls for large six eggs.

_____

8. The scarecrow had on a big, old straw hat.

_____

9. Sally has two beautiful blue eyes.

_____

10. Jonathon asked for blue, small erasers.

_____

(Answers are on page 87)

IDENTIFYING PREPOSITIONAL PHRASES

L.4.1.E Form and use prepositional phrases.

Common Prepositions: about, above, across, after, against, along, around, at, before, behind, beneath, beside, between, during, except, inside, near, outside, over, past, through, toward, under, until, up, with, without

A prepositional phrase is a phrase beginning with a preposition, its object, which is usually a noun or a pronoun, and any modifiers of the object, as in *he took a long walk **beside the lake***.

Directions: Read the sentences below and underline the prepositional phrases. The first one has been done for you.

1. The clues were found beneath the bridge.

2. As the kids walked behind the building, they found a lost dog.

3. Please walk past the pharmacy to get to the deli.

4. The boy had a really bad dream during the night.

5. Without a car, the man wasn't able to get to work.

6. She loved ice skating across the pond.

7. The girl had to button her coat as she walked against the wind.

8. We were so lucky because we got to watch a movie during lunch.

9. We trudged up the mountain toward the ski lodge.

10. The boat sailed silently over the winding river.

11. Sadly, she had to miss class and sit in the corner.

12. Beyond the sunset, you could see a palm tree on the beach.

13. Amelia was so excited to be going to a party at Mary's house.

14. Before the test, the students got to quickly look over their notes.

(Answers are on page 87)

FRAGMENTS, RUN-ONS, AND SENTENCES

> **L.4.1.F** Produce complete sentences, recognizing and correcting inappropriate fragments and run-ons.

A **fragment** is only a piece of a complete thought that has been punctuated like a sentence. Fragments can be phrases or dependent clauses or any incomplete word group. For example: *Walking to the store.* (This fragment is missing a subject.)

A **run-on** occurs when two sentences are run together without the proper punctuation and/or connecting words. For example: *Joe was happy about the raise he felt like celebrating.*

> A **sentence** has a subject and a verb and makes a complete thought. Another name for a sentence is an independent clause.

Part 1

Directions: Determine whether each group of words is a fragment, a run-on, or a complete sentence. Write *fragment*, *run-on*, or *sentence* on the line provided.

1. This morning after breakfast. _____

2. John, will you wash the car it really needs it? _____

3. Sara saw a dove in the backyard. _____

4. When Tommy saw the kitten. _____

5. Added paint to the picture. _____

6. He ate hotdogs he got sick. _____

7. When she saw her friend. _____

8. The girl saw her friend and she said hello to her. _____

Part 2

Directions: The sentences below are run-on sentences. Separate each run-on sentence into TWO complete sentences or use a comma and a conjunction to join the sentences.

1. He enjoyed playing football with his friends he hopes they invite him to play again.

   _____

   _____

2. It was a really hot day the boys decided to play in the pool.

   _____

   _____

3. Can you teach me how to sew the hole in my pants I have a hard time doing that.

   _____

   _____

4. The teacher read the story the students answered the questions.

   _____

   _____

5. How many pencils do you have I think I need to borrow one.

   _____

   _____

6. The cat climbed up the tree it sat there for two days.

   _____

   _____

7. Our dog ran away last night our neighbors found him in their backyard.

   _____

   _____

(Answers are on page 88)

USING FREQUENTLY CONFUSED WORDS

L.4.1.G Correctly use the frequently confused word (e.g., *to*, *too*, *two*, *there*, *their*, *they're*).

Part 1

Directions: Complete the sentences below by using the correct form of the homophones *to*, *too*, and *two*.

1. Have you been able _____ access the Internet today?

2. My brother will be turning _____ on Saturday.

3. We would love _____ have you visit us for the holidays!

4. I have that book, _____!

5. We took a nice vacation _____ Hawaii _____ years ago.

6. Are you sure you need _____ see the doctor?

7. _____ weeks ago, we learned about the planets in school.

8. I wonder if my friends will be able _____ attend my party!

9. The boy found out that all of his friends were going _____ the dance, and he wanted to go, _____.

10. When she went _____ the store, she purchased _____ gifts for the party.

Directions: Now it's your turn to write a few sentences. Write three original sentences on the following lines using the word indicated.

1. (to) _____

2. (two) _____

3. (too) _____

Part 2

Directions: Complete the sentences below by using the correct form of the homophones *there*, *their*, and *they're*.

1. I am so glad to have Sally and Maxine in my life. _____ my friends!

2. "Please go sit on the bench over _____!" ordered the coach.

3. Her parents picked up _____ new car from the dealership.

4. _____ is no soap in my bathroom; can you get me some?

5. I've met them before, but I can't remember _____ names.

6. _____ late! I really don't think _____ coming!

7. I wonder where my friends are! Oh! I see them over _____.

8. With all of the toys to choose from, the boys just couldn't make up _____ minds.

9. _____ two reasons why my answer is NO!!!

10. The teacher let her students start _____ homework in class.

Directions: Now it's your turn to write a few sentences. Write three original sentences on the following lines using the word indicated.

1. (there) _____

2. (their) _____

3. (they're) _____

Part 3

Directions: Circle the correct homophone to complete the sentences below.

1. My dad goes to the golf **course/coarse** every weekend.

2. The boy had to give the bus driver the **fair/fare**.

3. The **scent/cent/sent** of that candle is magnificent!

4. After the man's death, his family was in **morning/mourning**.

5. Our **principal/principle** has an office in the corner of the school.

6. The lion was carefully looking for its **prey/pray**.

7. Let's try to get to the **route/root** of the problem.

8. The **seam/seem** on the dress needs to be repaired.

9. The structure of the building is made of **steal/steel**.

10. She tied a beautiful scarf around her **waist/waste**.

(Answers are on page 88)

CAPITALIZATION PRACTICE

L.4.2.A Use correct capitalization.

Below are the basic rules for capitalization:

- the first word of a sentence
- "I"
- days, months, and holidays
- names of people and places, titles of people
- buildings and other structures
- organizations and other groups of people
- historical events and documents
- titles of books, games, newspapers, magazines, movies, plays, television shows, works of art, and so on.

Part 1

Directions: Read each sentence carefully and circle the words that need to be capitalized.

1. my family is going to johnny's birthday party at fun palace.

2. my friend annie and her mom took the whole family to france last summer.

3. sandy wasn't feeling well so she decided to visit dr. chen.

4. louise thinks having her birthday in december is awesome!!

5. emily is doing a charity walk, and all money will go to paws for pets!

6. have you ever read the book *charlotte's web* by e.b. white?

7. my grandfather fought in world war II.

8. pablo picasso is a famous artist who was born on october 25, 1881 in malaga, spain.

9. the *titanic* sank on april 15, 1912 in the atlantic ocean.

10. on sunday, my family will go to st. brendan's church.

Part 2

Directions: Rewrite the sentences below using correct capitalization.

1. the city of montgomery is the capital of alabama.

   _____

2. jennifer and patrick will travel to russia to work in an orphanage.

   _____

3. the trenton elementary school band will perform "yankee doodle."

   _____

4. nicole likes pepsi, but valerie and bethany prefer coke.

   _____

5. are you going to go to jennifer's party on saturday?

   _____

6. we celebrate st. patrick's day in march, not in october.

   _____

7. katherine planned a christmas party at lakeshore park this december.

   _____

(Answers are on page 89)

USING COMMAS AND QUOTATION MARKS IN DIRECT SPEECH

> **L.4.2.B** Use commas and quotation marks to mark direct speech and quotations from a text.

> A direct quotation presents the exact words of a speaker. A direct quotation is enclosed in quotation marks. The first word of a direct quotation is capitalized. The end punctuation (period, question mark, or exclamation point) appears before the ending quotation mark. Place a comma between other words in the sentence and the direct quotation.

Part 1: Direct Quotations

Directions: Add quotation marks and commas where needed.

Example: The zookeeper said, "Please keep your hands inside the bus at all times!"

1. Maryrose screamed I can't wait to travel to Disney World this summer!

2. She continued It's one of the happiest places on Earth!

3. Her friend, Lauren, asked Have you ever been there before, Maryrose?

4. Maryrose laughed Yes, over a dozen times, but I can't wait to go back!

A split quotation is divided into two parts. Begin and end both parts with quotation marks and be sure to capitalize and punctuate the first part the same way as a regular quotation.

Part 2: Split Quotations

Directions: Add quotation marks and commas where needed.

Example: "Kelly!" yelled Mom, "aren't you ready for school yet?"

1. Where are you going Lauren asked dressed up in your pretty dress?

2. I heard you took your science test today inquired Dad how do you think you did?

3. Oh boy said Mom the rough water of the ocean is what made your dad sick!

4. Oh Barbara said Dana do you really think you should get a pet crayfish?

5. The cat is purring said Mrs. Stanton which lets the owner know he's happy!

6. Ouch! Your dog just nipped me cried Jamie and I was only petting her!

7. I would like to introduce myself announced Denise I will be your substitute today!

8. Did you know asked Ashley that most of our planet is covered with water?

9. I really hope you put your dishes in the dishwasher yelled Mom I am not cleaning ONE more dish today!

10. Sara, I am so glad you came to my party screamed Natalie we are going to have so much fun!

(Answers are on page 90)

COMMAS AND COORDINATING CONJUNCTIONS

L4.2.C Use a comma before a coordinating conjunction in a compound sentence.

A compound sentence has two independent clauses or sentences. A conjunction is a joiner, a word that **connects** (conjoins) parts of a sentence. Here is a list of common conjunctions: *and*, *but*, *or*, *yet*, *for*, *nor*, and *so*.

When a coordinating conjunction connects two independent clauses, it is often (but not always) accompanied by a comma.

Example: John wants to play for his high school basketball team, **but** he's been having trouble keeping his grades up.

Directions: Read each set of independent clauses and create a compound sentence by using an appropriate coordinating conjunction.

1. Tom studied a lot. He didn't pass the test.

   _____

2. Maria was thirsty. She drank some water.

   _____

3. He was tired. He had a headache.

   _____

4. She put on a sweater. It was cold outside.

   _____

5. Grandma can't whistle. Grandma can sing.

_____

6. She can buy the book. She can borrow it from the library.

_____

7. The woman went on a diet. She gained weight!

_____

8. She doesn't drink milk. She doesn't eat butter.

_____

9. John reads the books. Steve reads magazines.

_____

10. Mary and Samantha left on the bus before I arrived. I did not see them at the bus station.

_____

11. We can go see a movie. We can get something to eat.

_____

12. John bought some new shoes. He wore them to the birthday party.

_____

(Answers are on page 90)

CORRECT SPELLING

L.4.2.D Spell grade-appropriate words correctly, consulting references as needed.

Directions: Read the four short passages and find the misspelled words and circle them. Write each of the misspelled words correctly on the lines below.

Tanya and Emily decided to sell tubs of chocolate chip cookie dogh at the annual school bake sale. There mom helped them compoze a signe for their booth that read "All Cookies: Buy Won, Get One Free." Peeple stoped by the booth all day long!! By the end of the day, they were completely sold out of cookie dough tubs. They were vary happy with themselves that they raized a lot of money for they're school.

1. _____   6. _____

2. _____   7. _____

3. _____   8. _____

4. _____   9. _____

5. _____   10. _____

The frist presidential election was in 1789. It wasn't realy much of an election. George Washington was the only person runing for president. He won. The same thing happened in 1792; no one ran against Washington. Since than, they're have been fifty-four presidential elections. In each one, two or more people have tryed to be elected president of the United States.

1. _____   4. _____

2. _____   5. _____

3. _____   6. _____

Did you no that Americans throw away about 50 billion food and drink cans evry year? They are taken to the dump to be covered by dirt. It may take a long time for some things to dicompose. Glass can be found in perfect condition after being buried for 4,000 years. Soon communitys will run out of places to bery their garbage. As a community we need to reduce, reuse, and recycle. Every person can make a diffrence.

1. _____   4. _____

2. _____   5. _____

3. _____   6. _____

Mr. Fox had not spoken for a long time. He had bin sitting quite still, his eyes clozed, not even hearing what the others were saying. Mrs. Fox new that he was tring desperately to think of a way out. And now, as she looked at him, she saw him stir himself and get slowly to his feet. He looked back at his wife. Their was a little spark of excitement danceing in his eyes.

1. _____   4. _____

2. _____   5. _____

3. _____   6. _____

(Answers are on page 91)

MORE SPELLING PRACTICE

L.4.2.D Spell grade-appropriate words correctly, consulting references as needed.

Directions: Read each sentence, looking closely for spelling errors. Cross out the misspelled words and write them correctly.

1. I can't wait to recieve the birthday gift from my grandparents.

2. The girl had a realy hard time finding her way to her classroom.

3. The teacher read a very intresting book to the class.

4. The dog had it's bone tucked under its paw.

5. The boy said, "I new my friend would help me out!"

6. Do you remember your frist day of third grade?

7. My friend has meny different kinds of pets.

8. The women we're trying to catch a bus.

9. Whould you like to attend the meeting with me?

10. The boy tryed to ride his bike, but he kept falling.

11. Did your best freind come to your party?

12. In Feburary, we celebrate Valentine's Day.

13. I hope you're parents will come on Saturday.

14. "What is your favurite color?" asked the art teacher.

15. My dad is so glad that our cusin can come to the graduation.

16. I think I ate to many cookies last night!

17. The girl bauwght the newest best seller book.

18. Finaly, the day our friends visit has arrived!!

19. "Can you here me talking to you?" Mom asked.

20. What a beatiful day to be hiking in the woods!

21. Will you be able to give me a diffrent tool to use?

22. Evry morning, Mom makes me pancakes for breakfast.

23. It's about time hour washing machine got fixed!

24. Dad siad, "I really wish you would tie your shoes!"

(Answers are on page 91)

WORD MEANING THROUGH CONTEXT

L.4.4.A Use context (e.g., definitions, examples, or restatements in text) as a clue to the meaning of word or phrase.

Directions: Read each sentence below. Circle the letter of the word that most closely matches the **bold** word in the sentence.

1. The sunset over the ocean was an **extraordinary** sight to see.

    Ⓐ dull   Ⓑ amazing   Ⓒ weird   Ⓓ sad

2. The man ran to get his umbrella since it was starting to **sprinkle**.

    Ⓐ downpour   Ⓑ snow   Ⓒ light rain   Ⓓ monsoon

3. When the girl gets embarrassed, her cheeks turn **scarlet**.

    Ⓐ red   Ⓑ itchy   Ⓒ blue   Ⓓ wrinkled

4. The farm had many animals, including a cute gray **burro**.

    Ⓐ giraffe   Ⓑ snake   Ⓒ snail   Ⓓ donkey

5. After a long day of adventure, the skiers made their **descent** from the mountain.

    Ⓐ going up   Ⓑ coming down   Ⓒ heading right   Ⓓ rise

6. She watched the players **collide** on the basketball court.

    Ⓐ crash   Ⓑ run   Ⓒ distract   Ⓓ blossom

7. The woman at the bank signed a very important **document**.

    Ⓐ dollar bill   Ⓑ paper   Ⓒ test   Ⓓ painting

8. The elderly man nearly passed out due to the **sweltering** temperatures.

   Ⓐ chilly   Ⓑ damp   Ⓒ hot   Ⓓ cool

9. The writing piece needed to be **revised** before it could be published.

   Ⓐ adjusted   Ⓑ made worse   Ⓒ ignored   Ⓓ harmed

10. The **committee** was in charge of making important business decisions.

    Ⓐ individual   Ⓑ group   Ⓒ one   Ⓓ class

11. Abby wanted to read her book before bed, but it kept making her **drowsy**.

    Ⓐ wide awake   Ⓑ very tired   Ⓒ scared   Ⓓ little

12. The bright lights on a car may **stun** animals while they run across the street.

    Ⓐ daze   Ⓑ bore   Ⓒ calm   Ⓓ cheer up

13. The kids at the party made such a **racket**, they were asked to leave and not come back!

    Ⓐ quiet   Ⓑ noise   Ⓒ silence   Ⓓ stillness

14. After the boy placed the final building block, his whole tower started to **topple** over!

    Ⓐ straighten   Ⓑ fall   Ⓒ bend   Ⓓ twist

15. The **feeble** man walked across the street very slowly.

    Ⓐ strong   Ⓑ energetic   Ⓒ weak   Ⓓ able

(Answers are on page 92)

GREEK AND LATIN ROOTS AND AFFIXES

L.4.4.B Use common, grade-appropriate Greek and Latin affixes and roots as clues to the meaning of the word (e.g., telegraph, photograph, autograph)

Part 1

Directions: Complete each sentence by using one word from the box below.

project	centimeter
portable	imported
thermometer	autograph
graphics	injection

The words in the box on the left have Greek and Latin roots. Some are formed from the Greek roots *graph* (meaning to write) and *meter* (meaning to measure). Others use the Latin roots *port* (meaning to carry) and *ject* (meaning to throw).

1. We admired the detailed _____ on the side of the sports car.

2. He really wished the heavy desk could move, but it just wasn't _____.

3. The teacher needed to _____ the map onto the wall so all of her students could see it.

4. "Please take out your _____ rulers so we can measure the shapes!" said Miss Cahill.

5. The line for the actor's _____ was three blocks long!

6. The nurse gave the patient a(n) _____, so her cut would heal.

7. After I felt my son's forehead, I ran to get the _____.

8. The cheese was _____ from France.

Part 2

Directions: Here are some more Greek and Latin affixes you may be familiar with. Can you think of familiar words that fit into each box?

quad- (Latin meaning four)	oct- (Greek meaning eight)
_____	_____
_____	_____
_____	_____

deca- (Greek meaning ten)	micro- (Greek meaning small)
_____	_____
_____	_____
_____	_____

uni- (Latin meaning one/single)	sub- (Latin meaning under/lower)
_____	_____
_____	_____
_____	_____

(Answers are on page 92)

FIGURATIVE LANGUAGE

L.4.5 Demonstrate an understanding of figurative language, word relationships, and nuances in word meanings.

An analogy is a comparison between two things that are usually thought to be different from each other, but that have something in common. Analogies help us to understand something because they are compared to something we already know. The first thing you must decide is what kind of relationship exists between each pair (i.e., synonyms, antonyms, homonyms, part-to-whole, time, place, age).

Example: Cold is to hot as up is to down. (The words are opposites.)

Directions: Read the analogies below, determine their relationship, and fill in the word that completes the analogy.

1. Mother is to father as sister is to _____.

2. Kitten is to cat as puppy is to _____.

3. Bat is to baseball as _____ is to hockey.

4. Heavy is to light as frigid is to _____.

5. Pork is to meat as broccoli is to _____.

6. Atlas is to maps as dictionary is to _____.

7. Long is to short as _____ is to narrow.

8. Spider is to web as bird is to _____.

9. Watch is to movie as _____ is to book.

10. Milk is to cow as egg is to _____.

11. Doctor is to hospital as teacher is to _____.

12. Dog is to paw as human is to _____.

13. Flamingo is to bird as _____ is to bear.

14. High is to low as _____ is to far.

15. Tired is to sleepy as _____ is to glad.

16. Paintbrush is to painter as _____ is to carpenter.

17. Hat is to head as _____ is to foot.

18. Cry is to sad as _____ is to mad.

19. Pail is to pale as hear is to _____.

20. Thermometer is to temperature as scale is to _____.

(Answers are on page 93)

SIMILES AND METAPHORS

L.4.5.A Explain the meaning of simple similes and metaphors (e.g., as pretty as a picture) in context.

Part 1

Directions: Read the following statements that contain metaphors in italics. Then complete the statements that explain the metaphors.

> Metaphors are comparisons that show how two things that are not alike in most ways are similar in one important way. Metaphors are a way of describing things.

1. *Brian was a wall*, bouncing every tennis ball over the net.

   This metaphor compares Brian to a wall because _____.
   - (A) he was very strong
   - (B) he was very tall
   - (C) he kept returning balls
   - (D) his body is made of cells

2. We would have had more pizzas to eat if *Tommy hadn't been such a hog.*

   Tommy was being compared to a hog because he _____.
   - (A) looked like a hog
   - (B) ate like a hog
   - (C) smelled like a hog
   - (D) was as smart as a hog

3. *Cindy was such a mule.* We couldn't get her to change her mind.

   The metaphor compares Cindy to a mule because she was _____.
   - (A) always eating oats
   - (B) able to do hard things
   - (C) raised on a farm
   - (D) very stubborn

4. The poor rat didn't have a chance. Our old cat, *a bolt of lightning,* caught his prey.

   The cat was compared to a bolt of lightning because he was _____.
   - (A) very fast
   - (B) very bright
   - (C) not fond of fleas
   - (D) very old

5. Even a child could carry my dog, Dogface, around for hours. *He's such a feather.*

   This metaphor implies that Dogface _____.
   - (A) is not cute
   - (B) looks like a bird
   - (C) is not heavy
   - (D) can fly

6. Sara always got straight A's in school. Her parents called her *the shining star* of Grant Elementary.

   This metaphor implies that Sara _____.
   - (A) wants to be an astronomer when she grows up
   - (B) is exceptionally smart
   - (C) likes the color neon yellow
   - (D) never studies for her exams

7. Now try to write some metaphors on your own?

   _____

   _____

   _____

Similes are comparisons that show how two things that are not alike in most ways are similar in one important way. Similes are a way to describe things. Authors use them to make their writing more interesting.

Part 2

Directions: Fill in the blanks below to complete the similes.

1. The bird was as _____ as a _____.

2. My Mom is as _____ as a _____.

3. The pillow was like a _____.

4. My puppy is like a _____.

5. The fire was as _____ as a _____.

6. Her baby blanket was as _____ as a _____.

7. The ice skating rink was like _____.

8. Snowflakes sparkled like _____.

9. He was as angry as a _____.

10. Molly crept into the room as _____ as a _____.

Part 3

Directions: Using the words below, create your own similes. Compare them to something that relates and paints a picture in the reader's mind.

1. hair

_____

2. clouds

_____

3. car

_____

4. grass

_____

5. rain

_____

6. puppy

_____

7. rainbow

_____

8. lightning

_____

9. popsicles

_____

10. classroom

_____

(Answers are on page 93)

IDIOMS, ADAGES, AND PROVERBS

L.4.5.B Recognize and explain the meaning of common idioms, adages, and proverbs.

Part 1

Directions: Match these idioms with their meanings. Break a leg!!

A.	Easy
B.	Go out and have a good time
C.	Dangerous situation
D.	Very sad
E.	Overcoming tiredness and feeling energetic
F.	Someone very special to you
G.	Follow the rules and win!
H.	Listen

1. Apple of your eye _____

2. Jungle out there _____

3. Second wind _____

4. Fair and square _____

5. Feeling blue _____

6. Paint the town red _____

7. Piece of cake _____

8. Lend an ear _____

> Idioms are phrases that mean something different from their literal meaning. They are common phrases or terms whose meaning is not real, but can be understood by their popular use.

NOW...select an idiom from above and write an original sentence!

_____

_____

_____

Part 2

Directions: Each sentence below contains an idiom. Determine the meaning
of the bold-faced idiom.

1. After playing six innings, the baseball team was **running out of steam**.

    _____

2. Since she was so tired from reading ten chapters in her science book, Jennifer decided
    to **hit the hay**.

    _____

3. Please **don't let the cat out the bag** about Kim's surprise party!

    _____

4. Sally accepted a job even though she had many other projects to complete in school.
    Her mom told her she was **biting off more than she could chew**.

    _____

5. Penny was feeling a little **under the weather**, so her dad suggested she stay home
    from school.

    _____

6. Mark was **on pins and needles** waiting for the results of his exam.

    _____

7. After Cecelia received the news about her job promotion, she was **on cloud nine**.

    _____

8. Before the talent show began, Amy had **butterflies in her stomach**.

    _____

9. I was worried as I ran through the airport to catch my flight to Florida. I boarded the plane
    in the nick of time.

    _____

10. Johnny had a sore throat, a runny nose, and couldn't stop sneezing! He was as **sick
    as a dog**!

    _____

(Answers are on page 94)

ENGLISH LANGUAGE ARTS PRACTICE TEST

Directions: Read the passage below and answer the questions that follow.

The California Gold Rush
by Kelli Dolan

Today, gold is one of the world's most valuable metals. The reason it is so valuable is because there is so little of it. The California Gold Rush took place between the years 1848–1858. Back then, gold hunters would carefully walk through streams and creeks searching for gold. If they were fortunate to find gold, they would seize it right away. Two famous gold hunters were James Marshall and John Sutter. James was building a sawmill for John Sutter when he found shiny flakes of gold in the river. The two men decided to stay quiet about their find since they didn't want to create a commotion that would then cause people to come to the area and search for gold. One man, Samuel Brannan, flaunted about where the gold was discovered and traveled to San Francisco to brag about the gold that James Marshall and John Sutter found.

Samuel Brannan invested much of his money on picks and shovels so miners could purchase them. He wanted the miners to have supplies when they went searching for gold. This then triggered thousands of people to flock to California in search of those glistening pieces of gold that could bring them a nice amount of money.

There were several people who did become rich. German miners located a sizable amount of gold that eventually produced gold worth close to $600 million today. The Murphy brothers also found gold in their first few days of mining. The gold they found, in just a year's time, was worth close to $40 million in today's dollars.

Just as miners became rich, there were others that were not as lucky. A man named Hiram Pierce from New York paid $25 for a sifter, but by the time he returned home about two years later, he was broke. He did write detailed descriptions about the difficult work of mining. Miners had to wade in bone-chilling waters as they moved dirt, often finding no gold.

The discovery of gold clearly changed the lives of many miners and their families. Fortunately, gold is still used today for many things. People around the world wear gold jewelry and collect gold coins. As long as gold is scarce, it will continue to be the world's most precious metal.

1. In the first paragraph of the passage, the author states "One man, Samuel Brannan, **flaunted** about where the gold was discovered and traveled to San Francisco to brag about the gold that James Marshall and John Sutter found." What is a synonym of the word *flaunted*?

   Ⓐ covered

   Ⓑ boasted

   Ⓒ joked

   Ⓓ concealed

2. What is the author's purpose for writing this passage?

   Ⓐ to persuade the reader to move to California

   Ⓑ to entertain the reader

   Ⓒ to inform the reader about the history of the Gold Rush

   Ⓓ none of the above

3. What is the main idea of the passage?

   Ⓐ The men who mined for gold sometimes didn't find any.

   Ⓑ Gold is a very valuable metal still used today.

   Ⓒ The work of mining was, at times, very difficult.

   Ⓓ The discovery of gold changed the lives of many miners and their families.

4. Reread this sentence from the passage: "This then triggered thousands of people to **flock** to California in search of those glistening pieces of gold that could bring them a nice amount of money."

   Use a complete sentence to explain what the word *flock* means.

   _____

   _____

   _____

5. Which is an OPINION about the California Gold Rush?

   Ⓐ James Marshall discovered the first flecks of gold in 1848.

   Ⓑ The miners should have had more expensive tools to find gold.

   Ⓒ Gold is used today in jewelry and coins.

   Ⓓ Hiram Pierce took detailed notes about the difficulties of mining.

Who Put the "Teddy" in Teddy Bear?
by Clifford Berryman

In 1902 America's then-president, Theodore "Teddy" Roosevelt, visited Mississippi to settle a disagreement between Mississippi and its neighboring state, Louisiana. While in the south, he went bear hunting with some of his friends and aides. His hunting party was joined by a group of newspaper reporters.

Members hunted for a few days, but they didn't capture any bears. Finally, on the last day of the hunt, Roosevelt's friends cornered a bear cub and presented it to the president as a sitting target. Teddy Roosevelt chose not to shoot the helpless animal: "Spare the bear. I will not shoot a tethered animal!" he exclaimed. A cartoonist, Clifford Berryman, either heard about or witnessed the president's act; he drew a black and white cartoon showing how the president refused to shoot the bear. This cartoon appeared in newspapers all over the country.

One married couple, the Michtoms, from Brooklyn, New York, saw the cartoon and were inspired by the president's action, or lack of action. Morris Michtom's wife created a stuffed bear with movable arms and legs. She and her husband placed the bears in the window of their candy store with a copy of the cartoon. The "Teddy" bears were a hit. The Michtoms wrote the president and received permission to use his name. The popularity of the teddy bears spread and soon they were being created in Germany as well.

Teddy bears are over 100 years old and are still popular with many children and adults. They are collected by many people; stamps and coins are the only items collected more.

6. According to the passage, Teddy Roosevelt didn't shoot the bear. Why didn't he shoot it? State your answer in a complete sentence.

   _____

   _____

7. The story explains that the Michtoms were **inspired** by the cartoon created by Clifford Berryman. What does the word *inspired* mean?

   Ⓐ   discouraged   Ⓒ   influenced

   Ⓑ   left alone   Ⓓ   chosen

8. In your opinion, how did the invention of the teddy bear change people's lives? Use details from the story to support your answer.

   _____

   _____

   _____

9. Underline the prepositional phrases in the following parts of the passage:

- This cartoon appeared in newspapers all over the country.

- In 1902 America's then-president, Theodore "Teddy" Roosevelt, visited Mississippi to settle a disagreement between Mississippi and its neighboring state, Louisiana.

- The popularity of the teddy bears spread and soon they were being created in Germany as well.

10. What can you infer about how teddy bears got their name? How do you know this?

_____

_____

_____

_____

Directions: Read the passage below and answer the questions that follow.

What Is Flag Day?
An excerpt from *American Flag* (Smithsonian Book)

It is the day to celebrate the American flag. It is held on June 14 because on that day in 1777, the Stars and Stripes became the official flag of the United States.

Flag Day started out as a celebration on local levels in the 1870s, including a national observance of Flag Day on June 14, 1877, the centennial of the flag. In 1885, a teacher in Wisconsin had his students write essays answering the question, "What does the flag mean to you?" After that the teacher, Bernard John Cigrand, wrote articles and made speeches encouraging Americans to fly flags and hold parades on June 14. In 1959, President Harry S. Truman signed an act of Congress making that day National Flag Day.

Flag Day is a good way to honor the flag and its history. Another U.S. holiday, Columbus Day, inspired something else connected to the flag—the Pledge of Allegiance.

11. The word *centennial* means how many years?
- Ⓐ 10 years
- Ⓑ 200 years
- Ⓒ 100 years
- Ⓓ 5 years

12. Who first began promoting the idea of setting aside a day to honor the United States national flag?

_____

13. What is the American flag's nickname? _____

14. Name an **antonym** for the word *encouraging*. _____

15. Just like the Wisconsin teacher, Bernard Cigrand, who asked his students, "What does the flag mean to you?" explain below what the flag means to YOU.

_____

_____

_____

Directions: Read the passage below and answer the questions that follow.

The Stag at the Pool

A thirsty Stag went down to a pool to drink. As he bent over the surface he saw his own reflection in the water, and was struck with admiration for his fine spreading antlers, but at the same time he felt nothing but disgust for the weakness and slenderness of his legs. While he stood there looking at himself, he was seen and attacked by a Lion; but in the chase which ensued, he soon drew away from his pursuer, and kept his lead as long as the ground over which he ran was open and free of trees. But coming presently to a wood, he was caught by his antlers in the branches, and fell a victim to the teeth and claws of his enemy. "Woe is me!" he cried with his last breath; "I despised my legs, which might have saved my life: but I gloried in my horns, and they have proved my ruin."

16. "I **despised** my legs, which might have saved my life: but I gloried in my horns, and they have proved my ruin." What does the word *despised* mean?
    Ⓐ adored   Ⓒ loved
    Ⓑ hated   Ⓓ cherished

17. What is the central idea of this fable?
    Ⓐ A stag was thirsty and came to the water for a drink.
    Ⓑ A lion chased the stag into the woods.
    Ⓒ The stag should have accepted himself for who he was.
    Ⓓ A lion interrupted the stag.

18. "But coming presently to a wood, he was caught by his antlers in the branches, and **fell a victim to the teeth and claws of his enemy**." Explain, in your own words, what happened to the stag.

_____

_____

_____

Directions: Read the passage below and answer the questions that follow.

The Lion and Mouse

A Lion lay asleep in the forest, his great head resting on his paws. A timid little Mouse came upon him unexpectedly, and in her fright and haste to get away, ran across the Lion's nose. Roused from his nap, the Lion laid his huge paw angrily on the tiny creature to kill her.

"Spare me!" begged the poor Mouse. "Please let me go and someday I will surely repay you."

The Lion was much amused to think that a Mouse could ever help him. But he was generous and finally let the Mouse go.

Some days later, while stalking his prey in the forest, the Lion was caught in the toils of a hunter's net. Unable to free himself, he filled the forest with his angry roaring. The Mouse knew the voice and quickly found the Lion struggling in the net. Running to one of the great ropes that bound him, she gnawed it until it parted, and soon the Lion was free.

"You laughed when I said I would repay you," said the Mouse. "Now you see that even a Mouse can help a Lion."

19. What is a central idea of this fable?
    - (A) The lion is the scariest animal in the world.
    - (B) It's easy to catch a lion.
    - (C) A little mouse can be a big help.
    - (D) It helps if everyone works together.

20. If you are **roused** from your sleep, what is happening to you?

_____

_____

_____

21. "Running to one of the great ropes that bound him [the Lion], she [the Mouse] **gnawed** it until it parted, and soon the Lion was free." What does the word *gnawed* mean in this sentence?

   Ⓐ   chewed   Ⓒ   quickly

   Ⓑ   hungry   Ⓓ   pinched

22. Who learned something in this fable—the mouse or the lion? What did he learn?

_____

_____

_____

Directions: Read the passage below and answer the questions that follow.

An Excerpt from *A Night at the Museum*
by Leslie Goldman

Larry sped to this meeting. It was in SoHo in downtown New York. He was running a little late, but luckily he found a great parking spot in front of his soon-to-be restaurant.

At that moment, it was a dingy, vacant, storefront but Larry had a vision. He had imagination. All he needed was money.

After climbing into his car, he placed a brown paper bag over the parking meter. Scrawled on the bag were the words "Broken Meter." This was a great way for Larry to get out of wasting change to pay for parking.

Soon he was giving his three potential investors a tour of the place. "If you'll turn to page one of your business plan," Larry said, trying to sound as official as possible, "you'll find the basic layout of the restaurant."

The men opened their folders to the first page. This wasn't exactly hard to do, because besides the cover, there *was* only one page in the business plan.

Larry explained what he thought was a brilliant plan, a sure moneymaker, and probably his best idea, yet. "We're going to go for an Asian fusion sort of thing," he said confidently. "There will be a sushi bar around the perimeter. Six shabu-shabu stations in the center here."

"Shabu-shabu?" asked one of the men. "We're dentists, Larry. Talk to us in English."

Larry said, "You sit around a pit of boiling water and cook your own food. It's very big in Japan."

The second man nodded, thinking about this. "Interactive dining. I like it. This is an interesting investment opportunity."

"I don't think we can go wrong," said Larry, clearly pleased.

23. "At that moment, it was a **dingy**, vacant, storefront but Larry had a vision. He had imagination." What is a synonym for the word *dingy* as it is used in this sentence?

Ⓐ tidy   Ⓒ clean

Ⓑ dirty   Ⓓ bright

24. Underline the **TWO** prepositional phrases in the following sentences.

"There will be a sushi bar around the perimeter.

Six shabu-shabu stations in the center here."

25. "After climbing into his car, he placed a brown paper bag over the parking meter. Scrawled on the bag were the words 'Broken Meter.' This was a great way for Larry to get out of wasting change to pay for parking."
After rereading this part, what can you infer about Larry's character?

_____

_____

_____

_____

_____

Directions: Read the passage below and answer the questions that follow.

An Excerpt from *Class Clown*
by Johanna Hurwitz

"Lucas is writing on his desk," a voice called out.

It was Cricket Kaufman, who sat in the seat across the aisle from Lucas. She was always spying on him.

"I am not," said Lucas, slipping his pen up the long sleeve of his shirt.

"Yes, you are," Cricket insisted. "I saw you do it."

Mrs. Hockaday came over to investigate. "Someone has written LC on this desk," she said, looking at Lucas.

"It could have been someone else. It didn't have to be me," Lucas pointed out.

"It is unlikely that someone else would bother to vandalize your desk with your initials," said Mrs. Hockaday.

"You didn't see me," Lucas protested.

"But I did," said Cricket proudly.

"Yeah? Well, it's your word against mine," Lucas said, turning to face the girl who always seemed to get him in trouble. As he turned, the pen fell out of his sleeve and onto the floor.

"See," said Cricket, pointing to it. "There's the proof."

Everyone in class knew that Cricket was planning to become a lawyer when she grew up. She practiced all the time.

Mrs. Hockaday sent Lucas out of the room to get some wet paper towels and soap from the boys' room. "I want you to wash that desk as well as you can," she told him.

Lucas grinned as he rubbed the desk. It was more fun doing that than social studies.

26. "It is unlikely that someone else would bother to **vandalize** your desk with your initials," said Mrs. Hockaday.

    What is a synonym for *vandalize*?
    - (A) clean
    - (B) broken
    - (C) destroy
    - (D) fix

27. Locate the two adverbs from the excerpt of *Class Clown*. Write them on the lines below.

    _____   _____

28. How would you describe Cricket's personality? Use evidence from the text to support your answer.

    _____

    _____

29. How does Lucas feel about school? Use evidence from the text to support your answer.

    _____

    _____

    _____

    _____

Directions: Read the passage below and answer the questions that follow.

The Kayak
Anonymous

Over the briny wave I go,
In spite of the weather, in spite of the snow:
What cares the hardy Eskimo?
In my little skiff, with paddle and lance,
I glide where the foaming billows dance.

Round me the sea-birds slip and soar;
Like me, they love the ocean's roar.
Sometimes a floating iceberg gleams
Above me with its melting streams;
Sometimes a rushing wave will fall
Down on my skiff and cover it all.

But what care I for a wave's attack?
With my paddle I right my little kayak,
And then its weight I speedily trim,
And over the water away I skim.

30. What word describes how the water is "behaving"?
    Ⓐ   smooth
    Ⓑ   calm
    Ⓒ   rough
    Ⓓ   peaceful

31. How do you think the kayaker feels about being in the water? Use evidence from the text to support your answer.

_____

_____

_____

32. What does the phrase, "foaming billows dance" in the first stanza describe?
    Ⓐ   the local Eskimos dancing around
    Ⓑ   the kayak being thrown around on the water
    Ⓒ   the birds flapping in the air
    Ⓓ   the water bubbling powerfully

Directions: Read the passage below and answer the questions that follow.

Monkey Adventure
by Kelli Dolan

There were two young, immature monkeys named Miles and Mickey who lived in the rainforest. They were constantly getting into mischief and always took advantage of the younger monkeys by swiping their bananas. They also played tricks on the elder monkeys.

One day, the group of monkeys held a meeting. Chief Monkey announced, "We're fed up with your antics, Miles and Mickey!"

"What are you implying, Chief?" Mickey asked.

"I'm not implying anything!" Chief Monkey said. "I am saying it rather clearly! We have had enough of you two! Why won't the two of you listen to anyone and why must you constantly defy rules around here? Go away and leave us in peace!"

Now, since both monkeys always wanted to travel, the monkeys replied together, "GREAT! We are totally ready to go!"

Miles always had ambition. He aspired to be Chief Monkey some day! He thought he might be able to learn new things from people, so he and Mickey hopped on a train and headed to the big city to start their new adventure!

As soon as they got off the train, they saw a bus marked "City Zoo." "Oooooo...sounds like fun!" cheered Mickey, "I wonder how much trouble we can get into here!"

33. What is a synonym for the word *defy*?
    - (A) obey
    - (B) follow directions
    - (C) cooperate
    - (D) disobey

34. Using the clues from the story about how the monkeys behaved at home in the rainforest, what kind of trouble could the monkeys get into while at the city zoo? Add a few sentences to complete the short story.

_____

_____

_____

_____

35. "They also played tricks on the **elder** monkeys." What do you think the word *elder* means?

_____

36. What genre is "Monkey Adventure"?

   (A)   realistic fiction   (C)   fable

   (B)   nonfiction   (D)   fantasy

37. Write a homophone for the following words in "Monkey Adventure."

   their   _____   new _____

   your   _____   here _____

   peace _____

38. If someone has **ambition**, they have

   (A)   motivation.   (C)   a lot of fun.

   (B)   very little self-esteem.   (D)   sleepless nights.

Directions: Read the passage below and answer the questions that follow.

Animals of the Ocean: Whales
by Judith Hodge

Scientists classify whales as belonging to a group of mammals known as cetaceans, which are large sea animals. There are at least seventy-five different kinds of cetaceans. They are divided into two main groups: toothed whales, which have teeth, and baleen whales, which don't have teeth.

Baleen whales have a set of plates which filter food out of the water. These plates, known as baleen, hang from the whale's upper jaw. Baleen is made of keratin, the same type of material found in human hair and fingernails. There are three groups of baleen whales: rorquals, which include some of the largest whales, right whales, and gray whales.

Toothed whales are generally smaller, with the exception of the sperm whale. There are sixty-five different kinds of toothed whales and they vary greatly in size and shape. Those more than thirteen to fifteen feet long are usually known as whales, while smaller species are known as dolphins and porpoises. Scientists classify dolphins and porpoises as toothed whales because they have the same basic body features, although most people consider them to be quite different.

Another difference between baleen whales and toothed whales is that baleen whales have two blowholes, while toothed whales have only one.

39. What is central idea of the passage?
    - Ⓐ Whales belong to large group of mammals known as cetaceans.
    - Ⓑ There are sixty-five different kinds of toothed whales.
    - Ⓒ All whales have at least one blowhole.
    - Ⓓ There are three groups of baleen whales.

40. According the passage, another word for large sea animals is _____.

41. What is the author's purpose of the previous passage?
    - Ⓐ to entertain
    - Ⓑ to persuade
    - Ⓒ to inform

42. What is the difference between a toothed whale and a baleen whale? State your response on the lines provided.

    _____

    _____

    _____

    _____

43. Dolphins and porpoises are considered_____ whales.

Directions: Read the passage below and answer the questions that follow.

An Excerpt from *Our Constitution*
by Linda Carlson Johnson

What makes the United States different from most other nations on Earth? You might answer, "We live in a free country." Or you might answer, "People in the United States have more rights than most other people."

But where do those ideas of freedom and the rights of people come from?

They come from a document called the United States Constitution. This document sets out rules for how our government works. And it lists important rights that U.S. citizens have by law.

The Constitution was written more than two hundred years ago by fifty-five men in a room in Philadelphia. The Constitution worked then because it had the support of Americans who believed in its idea of democracy that protects people's rights. The Constitution will continue to live and grow only as long as we cherish it.

Americans in 1787 didn't have TV or radio. But news that the Constitution was finished spread like wildfire. Everyone wanted to know what was this document that had taken so long to write. Within days, debate about the Constitution was raging all over America.

Some people argued that the strong national government described in the Constitution was a good idea. These people were called Federalists because they wanted a strong federal, or national government. Most people who lived along the Atlantic coastline were Federalists. These people's lives depended on trade with other nations and states, and they thought a strong national government would be good for business.

But many people didn't care about protecting trade. What they feared most was a powerful national government. These people, called Antifederalists, argued that the Constitution would take too many rights away from state governments and also from individual citizens. Many farmers who had claimed land in the western part of the United States, for example, feared that a strong national government would be able to take their land away.

44. What is the central idea of this passage?
   Ⓐ   People argued about whether or not the Constitution was a good idea.
   Ⓑ   Federalists wanted strong national government.
   Ⓒ   News of the Constitution spread rapidly.
   Ⓓ   The Constitution is an important document that protects people's rights.

45. "The Constitution will continue to live and grow only as long as we **cherish** it."
   What is a synonym for the word *cherish*?
   Ⓐ   treasure
   Ⓑ   neglect
   Ⓒ   dislike
   Ⓓ   mistreat

46. The people who argued that the Constitution would take away their rights were called

   _____.

47. "But news that the Constitution was finished **spread like wildfire**." What does the simile in this sentence compare?

   _____

   _____

   _____

48. During the time of the new Constitution, where were most farmers living?

_____

_____

49. Which statement is an OPINION about the United States Constitution?
   - (A) There should have been better ways to communicate about the Constitution.
   - (B) People across the United States felt differently about the Constitution.
   - (C) The Constitution is a set of rules for how our country should run.
   - (D) The Constitution was written by fifty-five men in Philadelphia.

50. What do you think life would be like if the United States didn't have a Constitution? Why do you feel this way?

_____

_____

_____

_____

_____

_____

(Answers are on pages 94–96)

ENGLISH LANGUAGE ARTS ANSWERS EXPLAINED

READING LITERATURE

Understanding Text (RL.4.1), pages 2–3

1. Bob is going to buy Jewel's foal. His parents gave him money and a bridle. He could use the money to buy the newborn horse.

2. Part A: The new advertisements highlight lower prices and possibly larger portion sizes.

   Part B: People commented that the prices were too steep for the size of the food servings.

3. Part A: Mary and Beth were really looking forward to a day in the park. I know this because of all the planning they did to make it perfect. It was an organized trip.

   Part B: It can be inferred that Mary was disappointed because it was raining. When you slump your shoulders, you are usually disappointed.

Summarizing Text (RL.4.2), pages 4–5

1. (B) The correct answer is B because the poem mentions "pillows at my head" and "lay a-bed."

2. The boy compared himself to a giant.

3. A counterpane is a bedspread or a blanket for your bed. The clues were **a-bed** and **pillows**.

4. Some of things the boy played with were toys. The poem mentions soldiers, boats, trees, and houses.

5. Answers will vary. He was happy since he got to play all day and he compared himself to a giant.

6. Answers will vary. This poem mostly likely took place in the past since today when kids are sick, they usually watch TV. Also, soldiers made out of lead are rare today.

Determining the Meaning of Words and Phrases (RL.4.4), pages 6–7

1. "Errands" can be replaced with the following words because they are all synonyms of errands: jobs, tasks, chores, duties.

2. "Prying" can be replaced with the following words because they are all synonyms of prying: snooping, being nosey.

3. "Peril" can be replaced with the following words because they are all synonyms of peril: danger, risk, hazard.

4. "Swift-rushing" can be replaced with "fast-moving" because it means the same thing.

5. "Treacherous" can be replaced with the following words because they are all synonyms of treacherous: dangerous, unsafe, risky.

6. "Sprang" can be replaced with the following words because they are each synonyms of sprang: jumped, leapt.

7. "Pangs" can be replaced with "pains" because they have the same meaning.

8. "Famished" can be replaced with the following words because they are all synonyms of famished: very hungry, starving.

9. "Herd" can be replaced with the following words because they are all synonyms of herd: a large group, crowd, pack, flock.

10. "Carcass" can be replaced with the following words because they are all synonyms of carcass: a dead body, skeleton, remains.

Answers will vary in Part 2 depending on synonyms used.

READING INFORMATIONAL TEXT

Understanding Text (RI.4.1), pages 8–9

1. **(A)** Choice A is the correct answer since the article is mostly about how the Statue of Liberty is a symbol of freedom. The other choices are only details stated in the article.

2. **(C)** Choice C is correct since *annually* means yearly.

3. **(B)** Choice B is the only opinion out of these four choices. The other three answer choices are facts that were mentioned in the article.

4. A possible answer: The broken shackles, which are hardly noticed, represent Lady Liberty destroying the chains of slavery.

5. **(B)** Choice B is the correct answer since the other choices are antonyms (opposites) of *restored*.

Explaining Text (RI.4.3), pages 10–11

1. Answers will vary but students should note some of the following differences:
   - The moon has no air, Earth has air.
   - Stars only shine at night on Earth, but on the moon, they shine all the time.
   - There is no weather on the moon, which is unlike Earth.

2. There is no air on the moon; therefore, there is no wind to disrupt the footprint.

3. Answers will vary.

Determining the Meaning of Words and Phrases (RI.4.4), pages 12–13

1. The word *bustling* means to move about quickly and busily.

2. A *gale* is a strong wind.

3. *Snarling* means threatening or wild.

4. If someone is *melancholy*, they are very sad.

5. The word *perilously* means dangerously.

6. If you are *ravenous*, you are very hungry.

7. If something just *commenced*, it just started.

WRITING

The Topic Sentence and Supporting Details (W.4.1, W.4.1.B), pages 14–15

Topic Sentence

Answers will vary, but here are some possibilities.

1. There are many species of spiders.

2. The United States is located on the continent of North America.

3. Every food group is important to providing essential daily nutrients.

Supporting Sentences

Answers will vary, but here are some possibilities.

1. **Students in public school should wear uniforms.**
   1. There would be no early morning decisions on what you should wear.
   2. There would be less bullying over who has the better/worse clothing.
   3. It would be cheaper for the parents since they wouldn't need to keep up with the current styles.
   4. Everyone would be the same, and no one would be better than the other based on their clothing.

2. **In order to keep kids healthy, schools should ban junk food.**
   1. Less sugar in kids' bodies allows them to work harder and be smarter while causing them to be not so hyper.
   2. Kids are able to have treats at home rather than snack all day in school and not eat a healthy meal for dinner.
   3. Students who play sports after school will benefit from a healthy diet during the day, allowing them to be more productive with their team.
   4. Foods that have no nutritional value do not aid in student attention.

3. **Dogs are awesome! They make the best pets!**
   1. People say dogs are loyal to their owners and will become part of the family.
   2. Taking care of a dog allows younger children to be more responsible.

3. Kids can play a variety of games and do activities with dogs that they can't do with other pets.

4. Dogs can be trained to help the family and have healing qualities. They are helpful pets.

Producing Clear and Coherent Writing (W.4.4), pages 16–17

This is an open-response question. Students should mention that Robert learns how important it is to be responsible.

Producing Clear and Coherent Writing (W.4.4), pages 18–19

This is an open-response question. Students should mention that the author feels that insects are very valuable and offer tools that help themselves and others. Students' opinions of insects will vary.

Describing Poetry (W.4.9.A), pages 20–21

1. The author refers to *he* in this poem. He is the wind.

2. (B) Choice B is the correct answer since the author explains to the reader the good and bad qualities of wind.

3. The wind brings good health because in the text it says that it "blows away sickness and brings good health."

4. The author refers to the wind as a friend because the wind is helpful and can do good things for others.

5. Answers will vary.

Describing a Story (W.4.9.A), pages 22–23

1. The word *admonition* means a warning. Harold was warned by his owners to take care of the house.

2. The narrator of the story is Harold.

3. The second sentence "I had been left home by the family…" is a clue. Also, the family spoke to him, "Take care of the house, Harold." Harold is speaking in his "I" voice.

4. An example of a synonym for *pelting* would be hitting.

5. An example of a synonym for *staked* would be claimed.

6. If you are looking *absently* at something, you are almost looking through it because your mind is drifting someplace else.

7. Chester is a cat.

8. The mood in the second passage is eerie or spooking. The author wrote that the wind was howling and the rain was pelting the window.

9. Answers will vary. It seems as if they both get along. Harold called Chester his friend.

Describing a Tale (W.4.9.A), pages 24–25

1. (A) Choice A is the correct answer since the author's purpose was to teach the reader a lesson about friendship and how important it is to have despite problems that may occur between two people.

2. (B) Choice B is correct since the word *determined* means the same as stubborn.

3. (D) Choice D is the correct answer since the overall message in this short story is friendship. The men had an argument, but the carpenter built a bridge to keep the men connected rather than a fence to the keep the men separated.

4. Answers will vary. Old Joe wasn't upset when the carpenter built a bridge because he had gotten his friend back.

5. Answers will vary. When the carpenter said he "had more bridges to build," he meant that he had more friendships to fix.

Describing Mood and Setting (W.4.9.A), pages 26–27

1. The setting is the beach because the author mentions waves breaking on the shore.

2. The author is creating an eerie or spooky mood in this short passage.

3. Some phrases that create that mood are: waves breaking on the shore, fog crept in, people who were dead, voices speaking, and so on.

4. Answers will vary.

5. Answers will vary.

Describing Informational Text (W.4.9.B), pages 28–29

Answers will vary, but here are some possibilities.

1. Milton Hershey was caring because he cared about children, even though he didn't have children of his own. He used the money he made to help others. One thing he did was create a school for disadvantaged children.

2. Milton felt that children were important and should go to school no matter how much money they had. He knew what it was like to grow up without money.

3. I think the Hershey Chocolate company is very successful. Whenever I go to the store, I always see their candy. I do think that the company will be successful in years to come.

4. I think "if at first you don't succeed, try and try again" means that if you make a mistake or mess up, try again and maybe the second time you'll get it right. Don't quit.

LANGUAGE

Grammar and the Use of Pronouns and Relative Adverbs (L.4.1.A), pages 30–31

Part 1

1. The gift (that) I got from my grandma needs to be exchanged.

2. My grandfather, (whom) I respect very much, was in World War II.

3. The grocery store no longer sells the cereal (that) I like.

4. The woman (whose) family moved away was very sad.

5. The young girl (who) lives down the street needs a babysitter.

6. We walked past the church in (which) I was married.

7. Butterflies, (which) have beautiful wings, enjoy the warm weather.

8. Last winter we traveled to Paris, (which) is in France.

9. The bus (that) I ride to school broke down on the side of the road.

10. My son, (who) is ten years old, just entered fifth grade.

11. What did you buy with the money (that) you received for Christmas?

12. Mrs. Thompson, (who) received the Teacher of the Year award, teaches in my school!

13. Your responses to the survey, (which) I received yesterday, were appreciated.

14. The little girl (who) is wearing the purple dress is my daughter.

15. The careless driver (who) raced through the red light received a ticket.

16. The car (that) was leased needed to be returned to the dealership.

Part 2

1. why	11. where
2. when	12. why
3. where	13. where
4. where	14. where
5. when	15. when
6. why	16. why
7. where	17. when
8. when	18. where
9. where	19. why
10. when	20. when

Using Progressive Verb Tenses (L.4.1.B), pages 32–33

Answers will vary, but check to see if correct progressive form is used in each sentence.

1. You should use the past tense in your response.

2. You should use the future tense in your response.

3. You should use the past tense in your response.

4. You should use the present tense in your response.

5. You should use the future tense in your response.

6. You should use the past tense in your response.

Using Modal Auxiliaries (L.4.1.C), pages 34–35

1. The boy looks pretty sick. I think he **should** go to a doctor.

2. Grandma has been driving all day. She **must** be exhausted!

3. "Mom, you **shouldn't** smoke so much. It's bad for your health."

4. The boy told the cashier, "Hi, I'm lost. **Can** you help me?"

5. You have such a beautiful voice. You **should** sing for us!

6. I know she speaks five languages, but **can** she speak French?

7. That brand new car looks very expensive. It **must** have cost a fortune!

8. Dad yelled, "I **can't** believe that you failed your test!"

9. "I'm on my way. I **should** be there in about 10 minutes," shouted Sally.

10. Even though I want that new bike, I **can't** afford it.

11. "**May** I please have another piece of cake, Mom?" asked Johnny.

12. Dad scolded, "You really **shouldn't** yell at your sister like that!"

13. You **shouldn't** talk loudly in the library.

14. She didn't feel well yesterday. She **shouldn't** be participating in soccer practice.

15. Call her now. She **may** be home.

Ordering Adjectives (L.4.1.D), pages 36–37

1. The boy has a **nice, oversized red** sweater. The size of the coat should come before the color of the coat.

2. CORRECT

3. They own a **short-handled, silver** steak knife. The size of the steak knife should come before the color of the steak knife.

4. She has a **round, yellow** dining room table. The shape of the table should come before the color of the table.

5. CORRECT

6. CORRECT

7. The recipe calls for **six large** eggs. The number of eggs should come before the size of the eggs.

8. The scarecrow had on an **old, big straw** hat. The opinion that the hat is old should come before the size of the hat.

9. CORRECT

10. Jonathon asked for **small, blue** erasers. The size of the erasers should come before the color of the erasers.

Identifying Prepositional Phrases (L.4.1.E), pages 38–39

Each correct answer is a phrase that begins with a preposition and includes its object.

1. The clues were found beneath the bridge.

2. As the kids walked behind the building, they found a lost dog.

3. Please walk past the pharmacy to get to the deli.

4. The boy had a really bad dream during the night.

5. Without a car, the man wasn't able to get to work.

6. She loved ice skating across the pond.

7. The girl had to button her coat as she walked against the wind.

8. We were so lucky because we got to watch a movie during lunch.

9. We trudged up the mountain toward the ski lodge.

10. The boat sailed silently over the winding river.

11. Sadly, she had to miss class and sit in the corner.

12. Beyond the sunset, you could see a palm tree on the beach.

13. Amelia was so excited to be going to a party at <u>Mary's house</u>.

14. <u>Before the test</u>, the students got to quickly look over their notes.

Fragments, Run-ons, and Sentences (L.4.1.F), pages 40–41

Part 1

1. Fragment—This sentence is incomplete. It is missing a subject and a verb.

2. Run-on—These are two complete sentences. (John, will you wash the car? It really needs it.)

3. Sentence—This is a complete sentence. It has both a subject and a verb and makes a complete thought.

4. Fragment—This is an incomplete thought.

5. Fragment—This sentence is incomplete. It is missing a subject.

6. Run-on—These are two sentences and should be separated by a period, or a coordinating conjunction can be added. ("He ate hotdogs. He got sick." or "He ate hotdogs, and he got sick.")

7. Fragment—This is an incomplete thought.

8. Run-on—These are two sentences. A comma needs to be added to separate the two sentences. (The girl saw her friend, and she said hello to her.)

Part 2

1. He enjoyed playing football with his friends**, and** he hopes they invite him to play again.

2. It was a really hot day**, so** the boys decided to play in the pool.

3. Can you teach me how to sew the hole in my pants**?** I have a hard time doing that.

4. The teacher read the story**, and** the students answered the questions.

5. How many pencils do you have **because** I think I need to borrow one.

6. The cat climbed up the tree**, and** it sat there for two days.

7. Our dog ran away last night**. Our** neighbors found him in their backyard.

Using Frequently Confused Words (L.4.1.G), pages 42–43

Part 1

1. Have you been able **to** access the Internet today?

2. My brother will be turning **two** on Saturday.

3. We would love **to** have you visit us for the holidays!

4. I have that book, **too**!

5. We took a nice vacation **to** Hawaii **two** years ago.

6. Are you sure you need **to** see the doctor?

7. **Two** weeks ago, we learned about the planets in school.

8. I wonder if my friends will be able **to** attend my party!

9. The boy found out that all of his friends were going **to** the dance, and he wanted to go, **too**.

10. When she went **to** the store, she purchased **two** gifts for the party.

Part 2

1. I am so glad to have Sally and Maxine in my life. **They're** my friends!

   Remember "they're" is the same as "they are."

2. "Please go sit on the bench over **there**!" ordered the coach.

3. Her parents picked up **their** new car from the dealership.

4. **There** is no soap in my bathroom; can you get me some?

5. I've met them before, but I can't remember **their** names.

6. **They're** late! I really don't think **they're** coming!

7. I wonder where my friends are! Oh! I see them over **there**.

8. With all of the toys to choose from, the boys just couldn't make up **their** minds.

9. **They're** two reasons why my answer is NO!

10. The teacher let her students start **their** homework in class.

Part 3

1. My dad goes to the golf **course** every weekend.
2. The boy had to give the bus driver the **fare**.
3. The **scent** of that candle is magnificent!
4. After the man's death, his family was in **mourning**.
5. Our **principal** has an office in the corner of the school.
6. The lion was carefully looking for its **prey**.
7. Let's try to get to the **root** of the problem.
8. The **seam** on the dress needs to be repaired.
9. The structure of the building is made of **steel**.
10. She tied a beautiful scarf around her **waist**.

Capitalization Practice (L.4.2.A), pages 44–45

Part 1

1. my family is going to johnny's birthday party at fun palace.

    "My" is the first word of the sentence, and it should be capitalized. "Johnny" is a person and "Fun Palace" is a place and both should be capitalized.

2. my friend annie and her mom took the whole family to france last summer.

    "My" is the first word of the sentence, and it should be capitalized. "Annie" is a person and "France" is a place and both should be capitalized.

3. sandy wasn't feeling well so she decided to visit dr. chen.

    "Sandy" is the first word of the sentence and a person, and should be capitalized. "Dr. Chen" is a person and should be capitalized.

4. louise thinks having her birthday in december is awesome!!

    "Louise" is a person and also the first word of the sentence and should be capitalized. "December" is a month, and months of the year are always capitalized.

5. emily is doing a charity walk, and all money will go to paws for pets!

    "Emily" is a person and also the first word of the sentence and it should be capitalized.

"Paws for Pets" is an organization and should be capitalized.

6. have you ever read the book charlotte's web by e.b. white?

    "Have" is the first word of the sentence and should be capitalized. "Charlotte's Web" is the title of a book and should be capitalized. "E.B. White" is a person and should be capitalized.

7. my grandfather fought in world war II.

    "My" is the first word of the sentence and it should be capitalized. "World War II" is a historical event and should be capitalized.

8. pablo picasso is a famous artist who was born on october 25, 1881, in malaga, spain.

    "Pablo Picasso" is a name and should be capitalized. "October" is a month, and months are always capitalized. "Malaga, Spain" is a place and should be capitalized.

9. the titanic sank on april 15, 1912 in the atlantic ocean.

    "The" is the first word of the sentence and should be capitalized. "Titanic" is the name of a structure and should be capitalized. "April" is a month, and months of the year are always capitalized. "Atlantic Ocean" is a place and should be capitalized.

10. on sunday, my family will go to st. brendan's church.

    "On" is the first word of the sentence and should be capitalized. "Sunday" is a day of the week, and days are always capitalized. "St. Brendan's Church" is the name of an organization and should be capitalized.

Part 2

1. **T**he city of **M**ontgomery is the capital of **A**labama.

    Montgomery is a city, and Alabama is a state. Cities and States are always capitalized.

2. **J**ennifer and **P**atrick will travel to **R**ussia to work in an orphanage.

    Jennifer and Patrick are both names, and names are always capitalized. Russia is a country, and countries are always capitalized.

3. The **T**renton **E**lementary **S**chool band will perform "**Y**ankee **D**oodle."

Trenton Elementary School is a place and should be capitalized. "Yankee Doodle" is the title of a song and should be capitalized.

4. **N**icole likes **P**epsi, but **V**alerie and **B**ethany prefer **C**oke.

   Nicole, Valerie, and Bethany are all names of people, and names are always capitalized. Pepsi and Coke are brand names, which are always capitalized.

5. **A**re you going to go to **J**ennifer's party on **S**aturday?

   Jennifer is the name of a person, and names are always capitalized. Saturday is a day of the week, and days of the week are always capitalized.

6. **W**e celebrate **S**t. **P**atrick's **D**ay in **M**arch, not **O**ctober.

   St. Patrick's Day is a holiday, and holidays are always capitalized. Both March and October should be capitalized because they are months.

7. **K**atherine planned a **C**hristmas party at **L**akeshore **P**ark this **D**ecember.

   Katherine is the name of a person, and names are always capitalized. Christmas is a holiday, and holidays are always capitalized. Lakeshore Park is the name of a place and should be capitalized. December is a month, and months are always capitalized.

Using Commas and Quotation Marks in Direct Speech (L.4.2.B), pages 46–47

Part 1: Direct Quotations

1. Maryrose screamed**,** "I can't wait to travel to Disney World this summer!"

2. She continued**,** "It's one of the happiest places on Earth!"

3. Her friend, Lauren, asked**,** "Have you ever been there before, Maryrose?"

4. Maryrose laughed**,** "Yes, over a dozen times, but I can't wait to go back!"

Part 2: Split Quotations

1. "Where are you going**,**" Lauren asked**,** "dressed up in your pretty dress?"

2. "I heard you took your science test today**,**" inquired Dad, "how do you think you did?"

3. "Oh boy**,**" said Mom**,** "the rough water of the ocean is what made your dad sick!"

4. "Oh**,**" Barbara said**,** "Dana, do you really think you should get a pet crayfish?"

5. "The cat is purring," said Mrs. Stanton**,** "which lets the owner know he's happy!"

6. "Ouch! Your dog just nipped me," cried Jamie**,** "and I was only petting her!"

7. "I would like to introduce myself," announced Denise**,** "I will be your substitute today!"

8. "Did you know**,**" asked Ashley**,** "that most of our planet is covered with water?"

9. "I really hope you put your dishes in the dishwasher**,**" yelled Mom, "I am not cleaning ONE more dish today!"

10. "Sara, I am so glad you came to my party**,**" screamed Natalie, "we are going to have so much fun!"

Commas and Coordinating Conjunctions (L.4.2.C), pages 48–49

1. Tom studied a lot, **but** he didn't pass the test.

2. Maria was thirsty, **so** she drank some water.

3. He was tired, **and** he had a headache.

4. She put a sweater on, **for** it was cold outside. *for* is used in place of *because*.

5. Grandma can't whistle, **yet** she can sing.

6. She can buy the book, **or** she can borrow it from the library.

7. The woman went on a diet, **yet** she gained weight!

8. She doesn't drink milk, **nor** does she eat butter.

9. John reads the books, **but** Steve reads magazines.

10. Mary and Samantha left on the bus before I arrived, **so** I did not see them at the bus station.

11. We can go see a movie, **or** we can get something to eat.

12. John bought some new shoes, **so** he wore them to the birthday party.

Tanya and Emily decided to sell tubs of chocolate chip cookie dogh at the annual school bake sale. There mom helped them compoze a signe for their booth that read "All Cookies: Buy Won, Get One Free." Peeple stoped by the booth all day long!! By the end of the day, they were completely sold out of cookie dough tubs. They were vary happy with themselves that they raized a lot of money for they're school.

1 dough	6. people
2. Their	7. stopped
3. compose	8. very
4. sign	9. raised
5. one	10. their

The frist presidential election was in 1789. It wasn't realy much of an election. George Washington was the only person runing for president. He won. The same thing happened in 1792; no one ran against Washington. Since than, they're have been fifty-four presidential elections. In each one, two or more people have tryed to be elected president of the United States.

1. first	4. then
2. really	5. there
3. running	6. tried

Did you no that Americans throw away about 50 billion food and drink cans evry year? They are taken to the dump to be covered by dirt. It may take a long time for some things to dicompose. Glass can be found in perfect condition after being buried for 4,000 years. Soon communitys will run out of places to bery their garbage. As a community we need to reduce, reuse, and recycle. Every person can make a diffrence.

1. know	4. communities
2. every	5. bury
3. decompose	6. difference

Mr. Fox had not spoken for a long time. He had bin sitting quite still, his eyes clozed, not even hearing what the others were saying. Mrs. Fox new that he was tring desperately to think of a way out. And now, as she looked at him, she saw him stir himself and get slowly to his feet. He looked back at his wife. Their was a little spark of excitement danceing in his eyes.

1. been	4. trying
2. closed	5. There
3. knew	6. dancing

1. I can't wait to ~~recieve~~ the birthday gift from my grandparents. **receive**

2. The girl had a ~~realy~~ hard time finding her way to her classroom. **really**

3. The teacher read a very ~~intresting~~ book to the class. **interesting**

4. The dog had ~~it's~~ bone tucked under its paw. **its**

5. The boy said, "I ~~new~~ my friend would help me out!" **knew**

6. Do you remember your ~~frist~~ day of third grade? **first**

7. My friend has ~~meny~~ different kinds of pets. **many**

8. The women ~~we're~~ trying to catch a bus. **were**

9. ~~Whould~~ you like to attend the meeting with me? **Would**

10. The boy ~~tryed~~ to ride his bike, but he kept falling. **tried**

11. Did your best ~~freind~~ come to your party? **friend**

12. In ~~Feburary~~, we celebrate Valentine's Day. **February**

13. I hope ~~you're~~ parents will come on Saturday. **your**

14. "What is your ~~favurite~~ color?" asked the art teacher. **favorite**

15. My dad is so glad that our ~~cusin~~ can come to the graduation. **cousin**

16. I think I ate ~~to~~ many cookies last night! **too**

17. The girl ~~bauwght~~ the newest best seller book. **bought**

18. ~~Finaly~~, the day our friends visit has arrived!! **Finally**

19. "Can you ~~here~~ me talking to you?" Mom asked. **hear**

20. What a ~~beatiful~~ day to be hiking in the woods! **beautiful**

21. Will you be able to give me a ~~diffrent~~ tool to use? **different**

22. ~~Evry~~ morning, Mom makes me pancakes for breakfast. **Every**

23. It's about time ~~hour~~ washing machine got fixed! **our**

24. Dad ~~siad~~, "I really wish you would tie your shoes!" **said**

Word Meaning Through Context (L.4.4.A), pages 54–55

1. (B) "Amazing" and "extraordinary" have similar meanings. Both express that something is wonderful. If you used "amazing" in this sentence, the meaning of the sentence would still be the same.

2. (C) A "sprinkle" means a small amount. "Light rain" can replace "sprinkle" in this sentence and the meaning would be the same.

3. (A) "Scarlet" and "red" are similar colors. If "red" was substituted in the sentence, the meaning would be the same.

4. (D) A "burro" is another name for a small donkey. If "donkey" was used in this sentence, it would have the same meaning.

5. (B) "Descent" means to decline. "Coming down" has the same meaning and would retain the meaning of the sentence.

6. (A) "Collide" means to crash into something. Therefore, "crash" could be used in its place in this sentence.

7. (B) A "document" is a piece of paper containing important information. "Paper" could also be used in this sentence and the meaning would be the same.

8. (C) "Sweltering" means boiling or extremely hot. "Hot" would also work in this sentence.

9. (A) When you *revise* something you change it. To *adjust* something also means to make a change. Both words have the same meaning and can be used in this sentence.

10. (B) A "committee" is a group of people. Therefore, "group" can also be used in this sentence.

11. (B) "Drowsy" and "very tired" have the same meaning. They both refer to falling asleep.

12. (A) To "stun" means to shock or daze. "Daze" can be used in this sentence, and the meaning would remain the same.

13. (B) "Racket" has the same meaning as "noise." "Noise" can be used in this sentence, and the meaning would remain the same.

14. (B) To "topple" means to "fall." Either can be used in this sentence, and the meaning would remain the same.

15. (C) "Feeble" and "weak" are synonyms. Either can be used in this sentence.

Greek and Latin Roots and Affixes (L.4.4.B), pages 56–57

Part 1

1. graphics—Includes the Greek root *graph*.
2. portable—Includes the Latin root *port*.
3. project—Includes the Latin root *ject*.
4. centimeter—Includes the Greek root *meter*.
5. autograph—Includes the Greek root *graph*.
6. injection—Includes the Latin root *ject*.
7. thermometer—Includes the Greek root *meter*.
8. imported—Includes the Latin root *port*.

Part 2

Possible answers

quad- (Latin meaning four): quadrilateral, quadrant

oct- (Greek meaning eight): octopus, octagon

deca- (Greek meaning ten): decade, decathlon

micro- (Greek meaning small): microscopic, microphone

uni- (Latin meaning one/single): uniform, unicycle

sub- (Latin meaning under/lower): submarine, submerge

1. Mother is to father as sister is to **brother**. (opposites)

2. Kitten is to cat as puppy is to **dog**. (baby animals)

3. Bat is to baseball as **stick** is to hockey. (object)

4. Heavy is to light as frigid is to **warm/hot**. (opposites)

5. Pork is to meat as broccoli is to **vegetable**. (type)

6. Atlas is to maps as dictionary is to **words**. (usage/object)

7. Long is to short as **wide** is to narrow. (opposites)

8. Spider is to web as bird is to **nest**. (usage/object)

9. Watch is to movie as **read** is to book. (action/object)

10. Milk is to cow as egg is to **chicken**. (item/purpose)

11. Doctor is to hospital as teacher is to **school**. (worker/location)

12. Dog is to paw as human is to **hand**. (item/purpose)

13. Flamingo is to bird as **grizzly/polar/koala** is to bear. (type)

14. High is to low as **near** is to far. (opposites)

15. Tired is to sleepy as **happy** is to glad. (synonyms)

16. Paintbrush is to painter as **hammer** is to carpenter. (tool/worker)

17. Hat is to head as **shoe** is to foot. (item/purpose)

18. Cry is to sad as **scream** is to mad. (sound/feeling)

19. Pail is to pale as hear is to **here**. (homophones)

20. Thermometer is to temperature as scale is to **weight**. (item/purpose)

Part 1

1. (C) Brian is compared to a wall because he kept returning balls, just as a wall would if a ball was thrown at it.

2. (B) Tommy is being compared to a hog because he ate a lot of pizza and hogs are known for eating a lot.

3. (D) Cindy is compared to a mule because she is stubborn and this is a characteristic of a mule.

4. (A) The cat was compared to a bolt of lightning because he was very fast, just like a lightning strike.

5. (C) Dogface the dog is compared to a feather because he is very light.

6. (B) Sara is compared to a shining star because she stands out among others. She shines above the rest just as a star shines in the sky.

7. Answers will vary.

Part 2

Answers will vary but see below for suggestions.

1. The bird was as **graceful** as a **ballerina**.

2. My Mom is as **little** as a **mouse**.

3. The pillow was like **a puffy cloud**.

4. My puppy is like **a ball of energy**.

5. The fire was as **hot** as a **volcano**.

6. Her baby blanket was as **soft** as a **sheep**.

7. The ice skating rink was like **an ice cube**.

8. Snowflakes sparkled like **dancing stars**.

9. He was as angry as a **bull ready to charge**.

10. Molly crept into the room as **quietly** as a **mouse**.

Part 3

Answers will vary but see below for suggestions.

1. Her hair is as golden as the sun.

2. The clouds were like pillows in the sky.

3. The car raced down the track as fast as lightning.

4. The grass in my backyard is as green as emeralds.

5. The rain is as cold as ice.

6. Our puppy is as happy as a clown.

7. The rainbow is as colorful as a bag of Skittles!!

8. Lightning is as scary as a monster.

9. The popsicles were sweet like a bag of sugar.

10. The classroom was as crazy as a circus.

Idioms, Adages, and Proverbs (L.4.5.B), pages 64–65

Part 1

1. (F) When you refer to someone as the apple of your eye, you mean that they are special to you.

2. (C) When something is referred to as a jungle, it is implied that it is dangerous and chaotic.

3. (E) Wen someone says they have a second wind, it means that they have a burst of energy.

4. (G) The term "fair and square" means that the rules were followed and the win was well earned.

5. (D) When someone if feeling blue, they are sad.

6. (B) The term "paint the town red" is used to describe a fun time.

7. (A) When something is said to be a piece of cake it means it is easy to do.

8. (H) To lend an ear is to listen to someone.

Part 2

1. getting tired. Running out of steam is another way to say you are getting tired or running out of energy.

2. time for sleep. To hit the hay means to go to bed.

3. keep a secret. Don't let the cat out of the bag is another way to ask someone to keep a secret.

4. took a job that was too big. When someone bites off more than they can chew, it means that they take on more than they can handle.

5. ill. When someone is under the weather, it means that they are sick (ill).

6. nervous. When someone is on pins and needles, it means that they are anxious or nervous.

7. so happy. To be on cloud nine, means that you are very happy.

8. nervous. When someone has butterflies in his stomach, it means that he is nervous about something.

9. just in time. In the nick of time means that something happened just in time or before time ran out.

10. so, so sick. When someone is as sick as a dog, they are very sick.

ENGLISH LANGUAGE ARTS PRACTICE TEST, pages 68–82

1. (B) *Flaunted* and *boasted* both mean to show off or brag about something. (L.4.5.C)

2. (C) This passage about California informs the reader about the history of the Gold Rush. (RI.4.8)

3. (B) The main idea of the passage is that gold is a very valuable metal that is still used today. (RI.4.2)

4. Answers will vary. According the passage, the word **flock** means a large group moving to a location. Large groups of people moved to California to search for gold. (RI.4.4)

5. (B) Miners SHOULD have had more expensive tools to find gold is an opinion. The other choices are facts about the Gold Rush. (RI.4.1)

6. Answers will vary. According to the passage, Teddy Roosevelt didn't shoot the bear because it was tethered and couldn't defend itself; therefore, the bear was helpless. (RI.4.3)

7. (C) *Inspired* and *influenced* both mean changing someone's mind or feelings about something. (RI.4.4)

8. Answers will vary. The invention of the teddy bear changed lives because they are col-

lected by many people and are popular with children as well as adults. (W.4.9)

9. This cartoon appeared in newspapers all over the country.

    In 1902 America's then-president, Theodore "Teddy" Roosevelt, visited Mississippi to settle a disagreement between Mississippi and its neighboring state, Louisiana.

    The popularity of the teddy bears spread and soon they were being created in Germany as well. (L.4.1.E)

10. Answers will vary. Students should be able to infer that teddy bears were named after President Roosevelt because his nickname was "Teddy." He also became known for refusing to shoot the bear that was tethered. (RI.4.1)

11. (C) Centennial means 100 years. (RI.4.4)

12. Bernard John Cigrand promoted the idea of setting aside a day to honor the U.S. national flag. He wrote articles and made speeches that encouraged Americans to fly flags and hold parades. (RI.4.1)

13. The American flag's nickname is Stars and Stripes. (RI.4.1)

14. One antonym for the word *encouraging* is *discouraging*. (L.4.5.C)

15. Answers will vary. (W.4.9)

16. (B) *Despised* and *hated* are both negative words showing how much you dislike someone or something. (RL.4.4)

17. (C) The central idea of the fable is that the stag should have accepted himself for who he was. (RL.4.2)

18. Answers will vary. Falling victim to the teeth and claws of his enemy means he was bitten, attacked, or even killed by the lion. (RL.4.3)

19. (C) The central idea of this fable is that even though a mouse is little, it can still be a big help. (RL.4.2)

20. Answers will vary. If you are *roused* from your sleep, it means you are woken up. (RL.4.4)

21. (A) *Gnawed* and *chewed* both describe ways something or someone eats. (RL.4.4)

22. Answers will vary. Students should see that the lion learned not to assume that just

because a mouse is small, it doesn't mean he can't be helpful. (W.4.9.A)

23. (B) *Dingy* and *dirty* both describe when something is not clean. (L.4.5.C)

24. "There will be a sushi bar around the perimeter. Six shabu-shabu stations in the center here." (L.4.1.E)

25. Answers will vary. The fact that Larry already had the brown paper bag in his car should lead the kids to believe that Larry has covered the meter before. Covering the meter with a "broken" sign when it isn't actually broken is dishonest. Based on this, students should infer that Larry is dishonest due to what he did. (W.4.8.A)

26. (C) *Vandalize* and *destroy* both mean to ruin something. (L.4.5.C)

27. Adverbs describe verbs. Two adverbs are *proudly* and *unlikely*. (L.4.1)

28. Answers will vary. Students should be able to identify that Cricket likes to tattle on Lucas. She may be described as annoying or bothersome. (W.4.9.A)

29. Answers will vary. Lucas appears bored in school since he was drawing on his desk. He appears to not be a very good listener either. At the end of the excerpt, he seemed happy that he had to wash his desk since he avoided doing social studies. (W.4.9.A)

30. (C) The water was *rough*. Words from the poem that show evidence of this: "ocean's roar," "rushing waves," "wave's attack." (RL.4.1)

31. Answers will vary. The kayaker appears to enjoy his time in the water. In the text it says, "Like me, they love the ocean's roar." (W.4.9.A)

32. (B) "Foaming billows dance" is referring to the kayak being thrown around on the water. (RL.4.1)

33. (D) *Defy* and *disobey* both mean someone is not listening to authority. (L.4.5.C)

34. Answers will vary here since students will add a few sentences about trouble the monkeys could get into at the zoo. (RL.4.1)

35. A word that means the same as *elder* would be *older*. (L.4.4)

36. (D) "Monkey Adventure" is *fantasy* since the events occurring in the story really couldn't happen. For example, monkeys talk! (RL.4.2)

37. Homophones: their—there; your—you're; peace—piece; new—knew; here—hear. (L.4.1.G)

38. (A) *Ambition* and *motivation* both mean to have a goal. (L.4.4)

39. (A) The passage discusses the various types of whales and that they all belong to the large group of mammals called cetaceans. (RI.4.2)

40. Another word for large sea animals is cetaceans. (L.4.5.C)

41. (C) The author is informing us/teaching us about whales. (RI.4.8)

42. Answers will vary. Students should conclude that toothed whales have teeth and baleen whales don't. Baleen whales have sets of plates in their mouths that filter food out of the water. (RI.4.1)

43. Dolphins and porpoises are considered toothed whales. (RI.4.1)

44. (D) The central idea of the passage is choice D since it is mostly about how the Constitution is an important document that protects people's rights. (RI.4.2)

45. (A) *Cherish* and *treasure* both mean to value something and have respect and love for something. (L.4.5.C)

46. Antifederalists argued that the Constitution would take away their rights. (RI.4.1)

47. Answers will vary. Students should be able to infer that when news spreads like wildfire, it is spreading very quickly and a lot of people hear about the news. (L.4.5.A)

48. Farmers were mostly living in the western part of the United States. (RI.4.1)

49. (A) There should have been better ways to communicate about the Constitution is an opinion; the other choices are all facts about the Constitution. (RI.4.1)

50. Answers will vary. Students should mention that if the United States didn't have the Constitution then we wouldn't have a strong government with rules and laws to follow. (W.4.1)

MATH

The Common Core mathematics standards are created to be building blocks between grade levels. The concepts learned in K–3 are foundational skills necessary for students to master grade 4 concepts. This allows teachers to make sure that achievement gaps are closed and that students have prior knowledge to continue their learning with more challenging concepts.

Each section presents a specific standard covered in grade 4 and provides the student with practice through a variety of question types.

UNDERSTANDING MULTIPLICATION

4.OA.A.1 Interpret a multiplication equation as a comparison, for example, interpret 35 = 5 × 7 as a statement that 35 is 5 times as many as 7 and 7 times as many as 5. Represent verbal statements of multiplicative comparisons as multiplication equations.

Directions: Write a matching multiplication equation and comparison statement.

	Comparison Statement	Multiplication Equation
1.	8 cups is 4 times as much as 2 cups.	
2.	40 birds is 5 times as many as 8 birds.	
3.		24 = 3 × 8
4.	42 days is 6 times longer than 7 days.	
5.	108 inches is 12 times the length of 9 inches.	
6.		36 = 9 × 4

Directions: Write a matching number sentence for each statement below.

7. Forty-two is six times as many as seven.

8. Twenty-eight is seven times as many as four.

Directions: For the story problems below, write a matching number sentence.

9. Ben has 6 puppies. His friend has 3 times as many puppies as Ben.
   How many puppies does his friend have?

10. I have twice as many cats as Pali. If Pali has 9 cats, how many cats do I have?

11. Sonali has invited 8 of her friends to a sleepover. She asked each of them
    to bring 3 stuffed animals.

    - Draw a picture of the total number of stuffed animals Sonali's friends will bring.
    - Write the equation that represents the drawing you created.
    - Solve for the number of stuffed animals Sonali's friends will bring.

    Equation: _____

    Solution: _____

12. Of the following pictures and number sentences, which is the same as
    12 is 3 times as many as 4?

    Ⓐ 21 = 3 × 7   Ⓒ 12 = 3 × 4

    Ⓑ   Ⓓ

13. Which of the following multiplication number sentences has the largest product?

    Ⓐ ? = 7 × 7   Ⓒ ? = 8 × 7

    Ⓑ ? = 6 × 9   Ⓓ ? = 11 × 5

Use the information below to answer questions 14 through 20.

Last spring, the Wildlife Reserve people saved baby herons, turtles, bullfrogs, thrushes, muskrats, and water snakes. The chart below shows how many baby animals were saved last spring.

Baby Animal	# of Baby Animals
Herons	7
Turtles	18
Bullfrogs	24
Thrushes	12
Muskrats	6
Water snakes	14

Directions: Fill in each blank with an animal's name or the number of animals to make each comparison statement true. Write a number sentence that matches the statement.

14. **Statement**: Three times as many _____ were saved as compared to muskrats.

    Multiplication Equation: _____

15. **Statement**: _____ as many water snakes were saved as compared to herons.

    Multiplication Equation: _____

16. **Statement**: There were _____ times as many thrushes saved as _____.

    Multiplication Equation: _____

17. **Statement**: The number of _____ saved was quadruple the number of muskrats saved.

    Multiplication Equation: _____

(Answers are on page 173)

SOLVING WORD PROBLEMS USING MULTIPLICATION AND DIVISION

4.OA.A.2 Multiply or divide to solve word problems involving multiplicative comparison, for example, by using drawings and equations with a symbol for the unknown number to represent the problem, distinguishing multiplicative comparison from additive comparison.

1. A turkey has 2 legs. How many legs do 54 turkeys have?

2. Alex scooped 240 pumpkin seeds from 8 pumpkins. If an equal number of seeds were scooped from each pumpkin, how many pumpkin seeds were in each pumpkin?

3. Ajay makes $36 in 3 months from selling homemade applesauce. If he sells the same amount of applesauce each day, how much does he make in one month? How much would he make in 9 months?

4. Abby harvested 180 bales of hay in 3 days. If the same number of bales is harvested each day, how many bales of hay did she harvest in one day?

5. Unknown Product: An apple cider donut costs $3. An apple pie costs 6 times as much. How much does the apple pie cost? Write a matching number sentence and solve.

6. Group Size Unknown: A hayride costs $15. That is 3 times more than the fee for the petting zoo. How much does it cost to get into the petting zoo? Write a matching number sentence and solve.

7. Number of Groups Unknown: A large bag of apples costs $18. A small bag costs $6. How many small bags could Albert buy for the price of a large bag? Write a matching number sentence and solve.

Demetri and his friends are having a pumpkin-growing contest. At the end of the season, each of them measured the distance around the widest part of their pumpkin (the circumference) and recorded the measurements in a table.

Below are clues to the size of each grower's pumpkin. Figure out the circumference of each pumpkin using the clues and record them in the table on the next page. Show your reasoning in the space provided in questions 13–17 for each clue.

Clue 1: Iron Man measures 2 times Soto's pumpkin.

Clue 2: Big Rock measures 4 inches more than Big Max.

Clue 3: Demetri's pumpkin measures 3 times Charisma.

Clue 4: Charisma measures 2 inches less than Aladdin.

Clue 5: Brandon's pumpkin measures 4 inches more than Big Max.

Clue 6: Aladdin measures 12 inches around the widest part.

Grower	Type of Pumpkin	Circumference of Pumpkin
Demetri	Big Max	8. _____ inches
Sean	Charisma	9. _____ inches
Evan	Iron Man	10. _____ inches
Brandon	Big Rock	11. _____ inches
Soto	Aladdin	12. _____ inches

13. Show/explain how you figured out the size of Aladdin.

14. Show/explain how you figured out the size of Charisma.

15. Show/explain how you figured out the size of Iron Man.

16. Show/explain how you figured out the size of Big Max.

17. Show/explain how you figured out the size of Big Rock.

18. Ainsley and Kaya are harvesting pumpkins and squash. They notice the pumpkin vines are 3 times as long as the squash vines. Place a check mark (✔) next to the pair of widths that describe the sizes of the vines.

☐ Pumpkin vine: 8 in
Squash vine: 24 in

☐ Pumpkin vine: 42 in
Squash vine: 36 in

☐ Pumpkin vine: 16 in
Squash vine: 4 in

☐ Pumpkin vine: 20 in
Squash vine: 5 in

☐ Pumpkin vine: 27 in
Squash vine: 9 in

☐ Pumpkin vine: 36 in
Squash vine: 32 in

☐ Pumpkin vine: 15 in
Squash vine: 5 in

☐ Pumpkin vine: 12 in
Squash vine: 3 in

☐ Pumpkin vine: 36 in
Squash vine: 12 in

19. More squash are harvested than pumpkins because it takes longer for pumpkins to grow. Ainsley and Kaya collected 7 times as many squash as pumpkins. If they collected more than 9 pumpkins, how many squash could they have collected? Solve and explain your thinking using words, numbers, and/or pictures.

20. At the end of the season, Demetri and Kaya were comparing their earnings from the harvest. Kaya said she earned $150. Demetri told her that he earned 3 times as much as she earned. She wondered how much he earned and went home to figure it out.

She used a bar model to show her thinking.

She first tried drawing it like this:

Kaya	$150		
Demetri	$50	$50	$50

But, she knew they didn't earn the same amount. What did she do wrong?

Part A. Explain what is wrong with her model.

Part B. How much did Demetri earn? How did you figure it out?

(Answers are on page 174)

SOLVING MULTI-STEP WORD PROBLEMS

4.OA.A.3 Solve multi-step word problems posed with whole numbers and having whole-number answers using the four operations, including problems in which remainders must be interpreted. Represent these problems using equations with a letter standing for the unknown quantity. Assess the reasonableness of answers using mental computation and estimation strategies including rounding.

Directions: Use the following information to answer questions 1–4.

Every year before school starts Kaya and her friends go shopping and then go to the movies.

The price of movie tickets has increased every year:

Year	Ticket Price
2011	$8.50
2012	$9.00
2013	$9.50
2014	$10.00
2015	$10.50

1. If Kaya had $34 for the movies, how many movie tickets could she buy in 2011?

2. If she had the same amount in 2012, $34, how many tickets could she buy in 2012?

3. How much did it cost for Kaya and 3 of her friends to go to the movies in 2012?

4. What was the difference in the cost of movie tickets between 2014
and 2011?

5. Ainsley wants to buy a pair of jeans that she spent several weeks saving for.
The jeans cost $102. If she saved $9 each week, how many weeks did it
take her to save enough to pay for the jeans? Explain how you figured it out.

6. Kathleen is buying goodie bag presents for her birthday party. She bought a bag of
candy that contains 30 chocolates. If she wants to put 4 chocolates in each goodie
bag, how many goodie bags will the 30 chocolates fill?

7. Mackenzie has $40.00 in her purse. Earrings are on sale for $6.00. How many pairs
of earrings can she buy?

(Answers are on page 175)

FACTORING
WHOLE NUMBERS

4.OA.B.4 Find all the factor pairs for a whole number in the range 1–100. Recognize that a whole number is a multiple of each of its factors. Determine whether a given whole number in the range 1–100 is a multiple of a given one-digit number. Determine whether a given whole number in the range 1–100 is prime or composite.

Directions: Questions 1–3 are based on the following information.

Dani and Jordyn are sorting the area of rectangles based on whether the area is prime or composite.

For questions 1 through 3, first, list all the possible whole-number dimensions the rectangles can have. Then, determine if the area of each rectangle is prime or composite.

1. Factors:

   Prime or Composite:

A = 12 sq yd

2. Factors:

   Prime or Composite:

A = 7 sq yd

3. Factors:

   Prime or Composite:

A = 29 sq yd

4. John and Dan sold baked goods at the bake sale. John made cookies and put them into packages that held 8 cookies each. Dan put his in packages that held 6 cookies each. They each sold more than 20 cookies. When they compared their amounts, they found that they had sold the same amount. What is the smallest amount of cookies John and Dan each could have sold?

5. Based on the information in question 4, list three possible amounts of cookies that John and Dan could have sold.

6. Explain how you chose the three possible amounts of cookies.

Directions: Questions 7 and 8 are based on the following information.

Lee was trying to find out how old Dani and Jordyn were, but rather than tell him their ages, they gave him the following clues:

- Jordyn's age is a factor of Dani's age.
- 35 is a multiple of both Jordyn's age and Dani's age.
- 21 is a multiple of Jordyn's age, but not Dani's age.
- The sum of their ages is 21.

7. What is Jordyn's age? Explain how you figured it out.

8. What is Dani's age? Explain how you figured it out.

(Answers are on page 176)

IDENTIFYING PATTERNS

4.OA.C.5 Generate a number or shape pattern that follows a given rule. Identify apparent features of the pattern that were not explicit in the rule itself.

1. Find the eighth shape in the pattern:

The eighth shape is _____ .

2. Explain how you figured it out.

3. Find the 10th number in the pattern below and write the rule.

2, 7, 12, 17, ...

4. Show the fifth step in the pattern by filling in the table below:

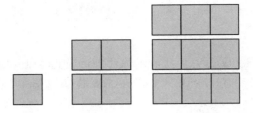

	Step 1	Step 2	Step 3	Step 4	Step 5	Step 6
# of pieces						
Rule						

5. What is the rule?

Patterns with Two Rules

Directions: Create a number or geometric pattern for the rules below and then explain your reasoning.

6. Rule: double the number and add 1.

7. Rule: reduce by half and then add 2.

(Answers are on page 176)

PLACE VALUE
AND DIVISION

> **4.NBT.A.1** Recognize that in a multidigit whole number, a digit in one place represents ten times what it represents in the place to its right.

Directions: Write the solutions for questions 1–3 and explain your reasoning in the space provided.

1. $800 \div 80 =$ _____

2. 300 equals how many tens? ____

3. How is the 8 in the number 2,386 similar to and different from the 8 in the number 2,836? Explain your reasoning.

First Game: Neil and David were playing number games. The game is to figure out how much greater one digit is in relation to the other.

4. Neil picked up a card with 56,739. David's card was 29,310.

   How many times greater is the 3 in David's card than the 3 in Neil's card?
   Use numbers, pictures, or words to explain your reasoning.

Second Game: Neil picked up a card with 47,312. David had to write a five-digit number that has only one 7 in it. The 7 is worth 10 times as much as the 7 in Neil's number.

5. What are three possible numbers that David could have written?

   _____; _____; and _____

   Explain using pictures, numbers, or words how you know the 7 in each number is worth 10 times as much as the 7 in Neil's number.

6. Look at the following cards:

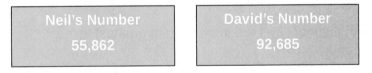

   Neil's Number
   55,862

   David's Number
   92,685

   Select the true statement(s).
   Ⓐ   The 6 in Neil's number has 10 times the value of the 6 in David's number.
   Ⓑ   The 8 in Neil's number has 10 times the value of the 8 in David's number.
   Ⓒ   The 2 in Neil's number has 10 times the value of the 2 in David's number.

   Use numbers, pictures, or words to show how the statement(s) is true.

(Answers are on page 176)

WORKING WITH MULTI-DIGIT NUMBERS

4.NBT.A.2 Read and write multi-digit whole numbers using base-10 numerals, number names, and expanded form. Compare two multi-digit numbers based on meanings of the digits in each place, using >, =, and < symbols to record the results of comparisons.

1. Write the following number using base-10 numerals.

   Five hundred twenty-three thousand, seven hundred eighty-nine

2. Circle the number with the smallest value.

   749,258   749,528   794,258   794,825

3. Underline the number with the greatest value.

   525,593   325,593   532,359   532,935

4. Select the sets of numbers that are in order from greatest to least.

   Ⓐ   632,594;   636,294;   634,836
   Ⓑ   629,273;   623,485;   621,485
   Ⓒ   632,304;   632,384;   632,275
   Ⓓ   629,384;   629,148;   629,284

5. Use >, <, and = to make each statement true.

   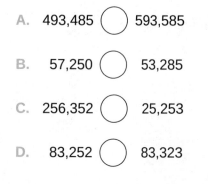

   A.   493,485 ◯ 593,585

   B.   57,250 ◯ 53,285

   C.   256,352 ◯ 25,253

   D.   83,252 ◯ 83,323

6. What is the largest number that can be made using these digits?

    5   4   8   3   1

    Explain using pictures, words, or numbers why this is the greatest number that can be made.

7. Complete the numbers to make each statement true.

    A. 25,295 < 25,__85

    B. 58,395 > __3,634

    C. 305,294 < 305,3__4

    D. 973,536 > 9__3,194

8. Is this statement true or false? Explain why.

    47,249 > 47,429

9. Nali read 4,367 pages in a year. Her sister Pali read 4,637 pages in the same year. Who read more? How do you know?

10. Write the following number in expanded form: 629,385.

(Answers are on page 177)

ROUNDING MULTI-DIGIT WHOLE NUMBERS

4.NBT.A.3 Use place value understanding to round multi-digit whole numbers to any place.

Directions: Complete the following rounding questions.

1. Place 1,739 on the number line below.

1,000   2,000

2. Round 1,739 to the nearest thousands and explain your reasoning.

3. The table below shows the population of Monarch Butterflies in the month of June for 3 years:

Monarch Butterflies in June 2014	Monarch Butterflies in June 2013	Monarch Butterflies in June 2012
148,779	107,033	123,737

When rounding the population of butterflies, Debbie said "When I round, I get the same answer." Her friend Jim said, "I disagree, I get all different numbers."

Can they both be correct? Explain your reasoning.

4. A number has been rounded to 800. What might the number be?
    Give three possible answers.

    _____ was rounded to the nearest _____.

    _____ was rounded to the nearest _____.

    _____ was rounded to the nearest _____.

5. Find two numbers that may be rounded and added together to make 150.
    What are the two numbers? Explain why you chose them and how they
    are a solution.

(Answers are on page 178)

ADDING AND SUBTRACTING MULTI-DIGIT NUMBERS

4.NBT.B.4 Fluently add and subtract multi-digit whole numbers using the standard algorithm.

Directions: Solve the following subtraction problems.

1. 6,295 – 4,596 =

2. Ben solved a math problem this way:

$$
\begin{array}{r}
492 \\
-256 \\
\hline
137
\end{array}
$$

Is his answer correct or incorrect? Use pictures, numbers, and words to show your reasoning.

3. Which number makes this sentence true?

6,404 – _____ = 3, 457

Ⓐ 3,567

Ⓑ 2,947

Ⓒ 1,947

Ⓓ 3,289

Directions: Use the following information to answer questions 4–6.

Suzie and James were researching animals. They found the following chart of animal weights

Animal	Weight in Pounds
Hippopotamus	2,297
Camel	1,885
Elephant	2,707
Buffalo	1,194
Bear	930

4. What is the difference in weight between the bear and camel? Show your work.

5. How much more does the camel weigh than the buffalo? Show your work.

6. Which animal pairs have a difference in weight that is closest to 1,500 pounds?
   - Ⓐ camel and hippopotamus
   - Ⓑ elephant and buffalo
   - Ⓒ elephant and camel
   - Ⓓ bear and hippopotamus

7. Solve this subtraction problem:

   4,387 – 2,754 =

8. Write another subtraction problem with the same difference as that in question 7. Explain how you figured it out.

(Answers are on page 178)

MULTIPLYING FOUR-DIGIT WHOLE NUMBERS

4.NBT.B.5 Multiply a whole number of up to four digits by a one-digit whole number, and multiply two two-digit numbers using strategies based on place value and the properties of operations. Illustrate and explain the calculation by using equations, rectangular arrays, and/or area models.

1. Mrs. Penza, the fourth-grade band teacher, is getting ready for the Spring Concert. The band members have sold 1,230 tickets to the concert. Each ticket costs $4. How much money will the band make from ticket sales? Write an equation to represent this story problem. Show your strategy and explain your thinking.

2. If the band has to set up all 1,230 chairs in the auditorium with 10 seats in each row, how many rows will they need? Show and explain your reasoning.

3. Mrs. Penza is wondering if it would be better to put 20 seats in each row. Joel says there would not be an even number of seats in all the rows. Is Joel correct? Using pictures, numbers, and/or words, defend your answer.

4. Fourteen parents of band members thought it would be a good idea to have a bake sale to support the band. They each made 3 dozen cookies. How many cookies did all the parents make in total? Show and explain your thinking using pictures, numbers, and/or words.

5. One of the parents wondered, if each of the 14 parents made 18 cookies, how many cookies would they have? Show and explain using a rectangular array how she could solve this problem.

6. What is another strategy she could use to find out how many cookies they made?

(Answers are on page 179)

DIVIDING FOUR-DIGIT WHOLE NUMBERS

4.NBT.B.6 Find whole-number quotients and remainders with up to four-digit dividends and one-digit divisors, using strategies based on place value, the properties of operations, and/or the relationship between multiplication and division. Illustrate and explain the calculation by using equations, rectangular arrays, and/or area models.

1. Jackson Hole Elementary School did a fundraiser to send their science teacher on a deep-sea exploration. She needed $3,744 for equipment, supplies, and travel expenses. There are 6 grades (Kindergarten–5) in the school. If each grade wanted to contribute an equal amount of money, how much does each grade need to raise? Show your strategy using pictures, words, or numbers.

2. How can you use multiplication to prove your solution to question 1 is correct?

3. Each grade decided to do a different fundraiser to raise its share. Kindergarten students decided to sell giant cookies for $2 each. How many cookies do they need to sell in order to raise their share? Show your strategy.

4. Grades 2 and 3 decided to sell tickets to a play they put on. If tickets
    cost $3 and they raised all the money they needed, how many tickets
    did they sell?

5. Grades 4 and 5 did a car wash. They raised $1,200 by offering wash/wax for
    $8 per car. They raised $800 by offering washes only for $5 per car. How many
    cars did they both wash and wax?

6. How many cars did they wash only?

7. Write a story problem for 102 ÷ 6, and show how you would solve the problem.

(Answers are on page 180)

EQUIVALENT FRACTIONS

> **4.NF.A.1** Explain why a fraction a/b is equivalent to a fraction (n × a)/(n × b) by using visual fraction models, with attention to how the number and size of the parts differ even though the two fractions themselves are the same size. Use this principle to recognize and generate equivalent fractions.

Directions: Questions 1–3 are based on the following information.

Evan and his sister Molly were laying tiles on the kitchen floor. They both covered the same area.

1. Evan laid a row of tile that looked like this:

   What fraction of the tiles is shaded?_____

2. Molly laid a row of tile that looked like this:

   What fraction of the tiles is shaded? _____

3. Evan says even though the number and size of the parts differ, the two fractions are equivalent, but Molly disagrees. Who is correct?

Directions: Questions 4–6 are based on the following information.

Evan and Molly decided to make muffins to celebrate all their hard work tiling the kitchen. They want to make batches of blueberry and chocolate chip muffins. They have two trays. The number of muffins each tray holds is different. They want $\frac{2}{3}$ of each tray to be filled with chocolate chip muffins.

4. How many cups does Evan need to fill with chocolate chip batter in his 6-cup tray? What fraction of Evan's tray is filled with chocolate chip cups?

5. How many cups does Molly need to fill with chocolate chip batter in her 12-cup tray? What fraction of Molly's tray is filled with chocolate chip cups?

6. Using numbers or words, explain how Evan's fraction and Molly's fraction are both equal to $\frac{2}{3}$.

Directions: Questions 7–9 are based on the following information.

Evan and Molly are making shelves for their rooms. Evan needs 5 shelves and Molly needs 10 shelves. If each of them uses a wooden plank that is the same length, show where they would make the cuts in their boards so Evan ends up with 5 shelves and Molly ends up with 10 shelves.

7. Evan's shelves: Show where the board will be cut so Evan ends up with 5 boards of equal length.

8. Molly's shelves: Show where the board will be cut so Molly ends up with 10 boards of equal length.

9. How do the size and number of Evan's and Molly's shelves differ? Do you see any equivalent fractions? If so, list them and explain how you know they are equivalent.

(Answers are on page 181)

COMPARING FRACTIONS

4.NF.A.2 Compare two fractions with different numerators and different denominators, for example, by creating common denominators or numerators or by comparing to a benchmark fraction such as $\frac{1}{2}$. Recognize that comparisons are valid only when the two fractions refer to the same whole. Record the results of comparisons with symbols >, =, or <, and justify the conclusions, for example, by using a visual fraction model.

Directions: Order the following fractions from least to greatest.

1. $\frac{5}{6}, \frac{1}{2}, \frac{7}{12}$

2. $\frac{2}{8}, \frac{11}{4}, \frac{6}{16}$

3. $\frac{9}{5}, 1\frac{1}{10}, \frac{8}{9}$

Directions: Given $\frac{5}{6}$ and $\frac{11}{3}$, answer questions 4 and 5.

4. Write an expression comparing these two fractions with $\frac{5}{12}$.

5. Find two fractions between $\frac{5}{6}$ and $\frac{11}{3}$. Explain how you know those two fractions fall between $\frac{5}{6}$ and $\frac{11}{3}$.

6. Circle the true inequalities:

$\frac{2}{3} < \frac{3}{4}$

$\frac{4}{10} > \frac{5}{8}$

$\frac{6}{8} < \frac{3}{8}$

$2\frac{3}{8} > 2\frac{4}{6}$

$\frac{4}{5} < \frac{1}{3}$

$\frac{7}{3} < \frac{4}{3}$

Directions: Questions 7–9 are based on the following information.

Jamie and Lauren are playing a game of fraction war. They pick 2 cards each and try to make the greatest fraction. If Jamie picked 7 and 10 and Lauren picked 12 and 6, answer the questions below.

7. What are the fractions Jamie can make? Which one is the greatest?

8. What are the fractions Lauren can make? Which one is the greatest?

9. Write an equation comparing the two largest fractions using a <, >, or =.

(Answers are on page 182)

WORKING WITH FRACTIONS

4.NF.B.3 Understand a fraction $\frac{a}{b}$ with $a > 1$ as a sum of $\frac{1}{b}$.

4.NF.B.3.A Understand addition and subtraction of fractions as joining and separating parts referring to the same whole.

4.NF.B.3.B Decompose a fraction into a sum of fractions with the same denominator in more than one way, recording each decomposition by an equation. Justify decompositions, e.g., by using a visual fraction model.

4.NF.B.3.C Add and subtract mixed numbers with like denominators, e.g., by replacing each mixed number with an equivalent fraction, and/or by using properties of operations and the relationship between addition and subtraction.

4.NF.B.3.D Solve word problems involving addition and subtraction of fractions referring to the same whole and having like denominators, e.g., by using visual fraction models and equations to represent the problem.

1. Select all the equations that are true. $\frac{7}{12}$ is equal to

   (A) $\frac{1}{12} + \frac{1}{12} + \frac{1}{12} + \frac{1}{12} + \frac{1}{12}$

   (B) $\frac{3}{12} + \frac{5}{12} + \frac{1}{12}$

   (C) $1 - \frac{5}{12}$

   (D) $\frac{9}{12} - \frac{1}{12} - \frac{1}{12}$

   (E) $1 - \frac{7}{12}$

2. Decompose the following fraction in two different ways to make the following using addition: $\frac{4}{6} =$

   Explain how you decomposed your fraction.

3. Jimmy and Kevin have $3\frac{1}{8}$ candy bars left over from the birthday party. After giving some to their friends, they have $1\frac{3}{8}$ left. How much of their candy bars did they give to their friends? Explain how you figured this out using a visual model.

4. If Jimmy and Kevin started with 5 candy bars, how much of the candy bars did they eat during the birthday party if they only have $3\frac{1}{8}$ left over? Write an equation to prove your answer. Show your thinking using a model, number line, or equation.

5. Max and Mia have two cakes left over from the birthday party. The cakes were the same size. The first cake has $\frac{1}{2}$ left. The second cake has $\frac{6}{10}$ left. Which cake has more left? Show or explain your thinking.

6. What is the difference in the amounts that are left?

7. Mia says that if the cakes were combined, they would make a whole cake. Max disagrees and says it would be more than a whole cake. Who do you think is correct? Prove that either Mia or Max is correct using a visual model or an equation.

8. Pax and Allan are helping to set up for a party. There are 7 glasses of lemonade filled $\frac{5}{6}$ of the way. Pax and Allan want as many of the cups to be full as possible. What fraction of the cups still needs to be filled for each to be completely full?

9. How many glasses would Pax and Allan be able to fill completely if 7 glasses are only filled $\frac{5}{6}$ of the way? Show your thinking using a visual model.

10. Some more of their friends came to the party, so now they need 9 full cups. How much more lemonade does Pax and Allan need in order to fill each glass?

11. Danielle, the birthday girl, has $\frac{17}{6}$ of her cakes left over. After giving some to her friends to take home, she has $\frac{9}{6}$ left. How much cake did Danielle send home with her friends? Use a model to show your thinking.

12. If Danielle started out with 4 full birthday cakes, how much cake was eaten at the party?

13. Danielle's mother says she can only keep 1 whole cake. How much does she still need to send home with her friends?

Directions: For each of the following, decide which is greater. Then, explain your reasoning using a visual model.

14. $\frac{7}{3} + \frac{1}{3}$ **or** $\frac{10}{3} - \frac{4}{3}$

15. $\frac{2}{9} + \frac{1}{9} + \frac{1}{9}$ **or** $\frac{3}{9} + \frac{2}{9}$

(Answers are on page 183)

MULTIPLYING FRACTIONS

1. The students at Singletary Elementary are going on a field trip to the aquarium. $\frac{3}{4}$ of the seats on a bus are filled. If one bus holds 60 students, how many students are going on the field trip? Show your thinking using a visual model.

2. Julia tried the above problem and solved it by first separating $\frac{3}{4}$ into three $\frac{1}{4}$s, then multiplying $\frac{1}{4}$ by 60 to get the solution of 15 students. Do you think Julia solved the problem correctly? Why or why not?

3. As part of the field trip, each student gets $\frac{2}{3}$ of a foot-long roll of gum. Steve, Tony, and Ben decided to combine theirs. Which of the following equations could you use to show what they did with numbers?

    Ⓐ $\frac{2}{3} + 3$

    Ⓑ $\frac{2}{3} + \frac{2}{3} + \frac{2}{3}$

    Ⓒ $\frac{1}{3} + \frac{1}{3} + \frac{1}{3} + \frac{1}{3} + \frac{1}{3} + \frac{1}{3}$

    Ⓓ $\frac{2}{3} \times 3$

    Ⓔ $3 - \frac{2}{3}$

4. When the students arrived at the aquarium, each chaperone took one-fifth of the whole group. How many chaperones are there?

5. Jared was having a birthday party with dinosaurs as the theme. As he and his mom were making the birthday cake, he told his mom that $\frac{4}{10}$ was the same as $4 \times \frac{1}{10}$. Jared's mom looked confused. Do you agree with Jared? Explain your thinking with words and a number sentence.

As guests to Jared's party were arriving, each was offered a dinosaur mask. They had a choice of being a Stegosaurus, Tyrannosaurus rex, Pteradactyl, or Demetrodon.

One-half as many people wanted Stegosaurus masks as Demetrodon masks, one-fifth as many people wanted Demetrodon masks as wanted Pterodactyl masks, and one-half as many people wanted Pterodactyl masks as wanted Tyrannosaurus rex masks. If we know that 20 people wanted Tyrannosaurus rex masks, answer the following questions:

6. How many people asked to be Pterodactyl? Show and explain your thinking using pictures and numbers.

7. How many people asked to be Demetrodon? Show and explain your thinking using pictures and numbers.

8. How many people asked to be Stegosaurus? Show and explain your thinking using pictures and numbers.

9. Last week, Kaya ran 5 laps around the lake. Bridget ran $\frac{1}{5}$ as many laps around the lake as Kaya did. How many laps around the lake did Bridget run? Show your thinking using a visual model and equation.

10. Lucas has 6 cups of powdered sugar. He sprinkles $\frac{1}{6}$ of the sugar onto a plate of brownies and sprinkles the rest onto a plate of lemon cookies. How much sugar does Lucas sprinkle on the brownies and lemon cookies? Show your thinking using a visual model and equation.

11. Olivia picked 4 pounds of strawberries. That afternoon, Olivia's sister ate $\frac{3}{4}$ of the strawberries. How many pounds of strawberries did Olivia's sister eat? Show your thinking using a visual model and equation.

(Answers are on page 184)

EQUIVALENT FRACTIONS WITH DENOMINATORS OF 10 AND 100

4.NF.C.5 Express a fraction with denominator 10 as an equivalent fraction with denominator 100, and use this technique to add two fractions with respective denominators 10 and 100.

1. Standing in the lunch line, Ty and Terra were talking about money. They noticed a penny was $\frac{1}{100}$ of a dollar and a dime was $\frac{1}{10}$ of a dollar. Ty had 3 dimes and 5 pennies. What fraction of a dollar does Ty have? Write your solution in both fraction and decimal form. Use a model to show your thinking and explain in words.

2. Terra had 6 dimes and 2 pennies. What fraction of a dollar does Terra have? Write your solution in both fraction and decimal form. Use a model to show your thinking and explain in words.

3. After paying for lunch, Ty and Terra look at the change in their hands. Ty has 1 dime and 20 pennies and Terra has 4 dimes. Ty thinks he has more money than Terra because he has more coins. Do you agree or disagree? Explain and show your thinking.

4. The shaded area represents a value less than 1 whole.

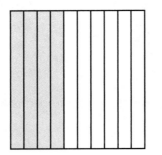

Select all of the values that are equivalent to the shaded area:

(A) $\frac{4}{10}$ (B) 0.04   (C) $\frac{40}{100}$ (D) 0.40   (E) $\frac{4}{100}$

5. Choose one of the solutions that you do not think is equivalent to the shaded area in Question 4. Explain why that fraction or decimal is not equivalent.

6. List three different ways the shaded value in the following figure can be expressed in fractional or decimal form.

7. The art club was painting a mural on the playground. The picture below shows how much of the mural is complete. Write a decimal that shows how much of the mural is complete.

(Answers are on page 186)

DECIMAL NOTATION AND FRACTIONS

Maya and Therese were playing a game with fractions and decimals. The game had two parts.

Part 1: Match the visual model with the fraction and decimal.

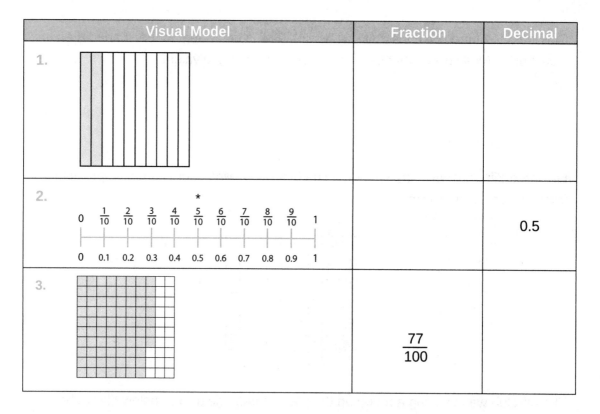

Visual Model	Fraction	Decimal
1.		
2.		0.5
3.	$\frac{77}{100}$	

4. Maya picked up a card with 0.40 on it. When she looked on the number line, she couldn't figure out where it went. Therese said it was the same as $\frac{4}{10}$. Is she correct? Explain why or why not.

5. What would the visual model of 0.40 look like on a grid?

Part 2: Is the equation true?

6. 3 hundredths + 5 tenths = .35

   Is this equation true? Explain your reasoning.

7. $0.40 + 0.3 = \dfrac{70}{100}$

   Is this equation true? Explain your reasoning.

8. 27 hundredths = 2 tenths + 7 hundredths

   Is this equation true? Explain your reasoning.

(Answers are on page 187)

COMPARING DECIMALS

4.NF.C.7 Compare two decimals to hundredths by reasoning about their size. Recognize that comparisons are valid only when the two decimals refer to the same whole. Record the results of comparisons with the symbols >, =, or <, and justify the conclusions, for example by using a visual model.

Directions: Compare the following decimals and explain your reasoning.

Fill in the blank using the symbols >, <, or =	Explain your thinking using words and a visual model
1. 3.2 ◯ 3.20	
2. 56.3 ◯ 56.43	
3. 0.9 ◯ 0.09	

4. David and Goliath were recording the amount it rained in a rain gauge. In the first week, it rained 1.25 inches. The second week the rain gauge read 1.4 inches, and the third week it rained 0.7 inches. Which week did it rain the least? Explain your thinking.

5. During the fourth week it rained less than 1.5 inches, but more than the amount it rained the first week (1.25 inches). What is the possible amount it could have rained the fourth week?

6. Goliath says it rained more the second week than the first. David disagrees because he says that 1.25 inches has more numbers than 1.4 inches, so it is greater, and it rained more the first week. Who do you think is correct? Justify your answer with a visual model and a written explanation.

Directions: Place the numbers on the number line and write a comparison using >, =, <.

7. 49.7 ◯ 49.77

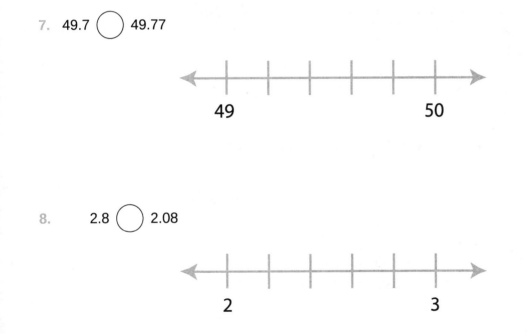

8. 2.8 ◯ 2.08

(Answers are on page 188)

UNITS OF MEASURE

Ben was doing research on sharks and created the following chart to show the information. He wrote the shark height in feet. Complete the chart to show the length of each shark in inches.

Type of Shark	Feet	Inches
1. Great White Shark	20	
2. Tiger Shark	10	
3. Lemon Shark	9	
4. Shortfin Mako Shark	13	
5. Bull Shark	7	
6. Great Hammerhead Shark	12	

7. Describe how the sharks' length in feet relates to their length in inches.

8. Ben's sister Rebecca tells him the Great Hammerhead Shark is actually 4 yards long. Ben disagrees. Who is correct? Explain your thinking using words, numbers, and/or pictures.

9. Ben's brother Brad was conducting a science experiment using a water slide he had just designed. He would have different people go down the slide on a tube and measure how far they traveled. When he was recording the units, he wrote:

Johnny went a distance of 3 _____ (or 36 _____).

Fill in the blanks using the Unit Bank below.

Unit Bank	
Millimeters	Meters
Inches	Feet
Yards	Centimeters

10. If Brad had written 5 *centimeters* (or 500 *meters*) for the distance Kim slid past the slide, would those be reasonable units for him to record? Explain why or why not.

11. Brad clocked the amount of time it took each participant to conduct three rounds of the water slide experiment. The chart below shows the times he recorded:

Jill	$\frac{1}{2}$ hour
John	3,600 seconds
Jack	40 minutes
Julius	$\frac{3}{5}$ hour
Justin	5,400 seconds

List the students from slowest to fastest and explain your thinking.

Directions: Questions 12–15 are based on the following information.

Essence and her mother were dropping off some bedding at the dry cleaners. The lady behind the counter placed each piece of bedding on the scale to weigh them.

The weights in kilograms are listed in the chart below.

Fill in the rest of the chart to show how much each piece of bedding weighs in grams.

	Metric Weight	
	Kilograms	**Grams**
12.	24	
13.	9	
14.	17	
15.	5	

Directions: Questions 16–18 are based on the following information.

After leaving the dry cleaners, Essence and her mother went to the grocery store. As they were weighing the vegetables, she noticed the scale said pounds and ounces. Next to it, there was a chart (shown below). Fill in the missing information.

Standard Weight	
Pounds	**Ounces**
1	16
2	
3	
4	

16.

17.

18.

19. How much does the bag of potatoes weigh in ounces if it weighs $4\frac{1}{2}$ pounds?

20. Explain the relationship between pounds and ounces using pictures, words, or numbers.

(Answers are on page 189)

145

WORD PROBLEMS INVOLVING MEASUREMENTS

> **4.MD.A.2** Use the four operations to solve word problems that involve distances, intervals of time, liquid volumes, masses of objects, and money, including problems involving simple fractions or decimals, and problems that require expressing measurements given in a larger unit in terms of a smaller unit. Represent measurement quantities using diagrams such as number line diagrams that feature a measurement scale.

1. Jay does extra chores around the house to earn money from his parents. He gets a quarter for each window he cleans, a nickel for each dish he washes, and a dime for each dish he dries and puts away. If Jay cleans 6 windows, washes 18 dishes, and dries and puts away 15 dishes, how many dollars will he earn?

2. Jay received 5 dollars from his parents for the chores he did. If he washed, dried, and put away 20 dishes, how many windows did he clean?

3. Sean and Jackson are competing in the long-jump together. Sean jumped 10.5 feet. Jackson jumped $3\frac{3}{4}$ feet farther than Sean. How far did Jackson jump? On a number line, show how far Sean and Jackson jumped.

4. How many feet would Sean have to jump to beat Jackson by $4\frac{1}{4}$ feet?

5. Evan, Sam, Zach, and Stevie are in a band. Evan wrote a song that is 150 seconds long. Sam and Stevie worked together to write a song that is $2\frac{1}{2}$ minutes long. Zach's song is 3 minutes and 20 seconds long. If they put all the songs together on a CD, how many minutes long will it be?

6. If they practice for a concert, and their set is 10 minutes long, how much longer did they take to play at the concert than on their CD?

7. Demetri and Kaya are making smoothies. They need a quart of yogurt for every four servings of smoothies. How many quarts of yogurt do they need for 6 servings of smoothies?

8. How many servings can they make with a gallon of yogurt?

(Answers are on page 190)

FINDING AREA
AND PERIMETER

> **4.MD.A.3** Apply the area and perimeter formulas for rectangles in real world and mathematical problems. For example, find the width of a rectangular room given the area of the flooring and the length, by viewing the area formula as a multiplication equation with an unknown factor.

Directions: Questions 1–3 are based on the following information.

Mrs. Adams' class was making a mural to hang in the cafeteria. They used one-inch tiles to create a mural that measured 8 feet long and 10 feet wide.

In order to have everyone working on the mural, they decided to split it into three sections. Here are the sections and their measurements:

- **Section 1:**
  - Rectangle
  - Length is 1 foot more than width

- **Section 2:**
  - Square
  - Perimeter is 12 feet

- **Section 3:**
  - Rectangle
  - Area is 15 square feet

For questions 1 through 3, find the perimeter or area of each section.

1. Section 1: Perimeter = _____

   Explain your thinking using equations, pictures, and words.

2. Section 2: Area = _____

   Explain your thinking using equations, pictures, and words.

3. Section 3: Perimeter = _____

   Explain your thinking using equations, pictures, and words.

4. If they doubled the length and width of the 8 feet × 10 feet mural, would the perimeter and area also be doubled? Show and explain what happens to the perimeter.

5. The class decided to make another mural. If they want the area of the mural to be 24 feet and the length to be 4 feet, what does the width need to be?

(Answers are on page 191)

LINE PLOTS

4.MD.B.4 Make a line plot to display a data set of measurements in fractions of a unit ($\frac{1}{2}$, $\frac{1}{4}$, $\frac{1}{8}$). Solve problems involving addition and subtraction of fractions by using information presented in line plots.

In the spring, Mr. Rodriguez's class planted bean seeds in small cups. Each day, students watered and took care of the seeds. After 10 days, they measured the height of their plants to the nearest quarter inch.

Here are the measurements from one group:

Ella = $3\frac{3}{4}$ in   Max = 4 in   Sammy = 4 in

Shawn = $5\frac{1}{4}$ in   Gloria = $4\frac{1}{4}$ in   Victoria = $4\frac{2}{4}$ in

Mia = $4\frac{2}{4}$ in   Mitch = $5\frac{1}{4}$ in   Carmen = $4\frac{2}{4}$ in

Samantha = 5 in   Ron = $4\frac{2}{4}$ in   Justin = $3\frac{3}{4}$ in

Using a ruler, help two more students measure their plants with the given ruler, and add their data to the line plot you will create in question 3.

1. What is Adam's plant length?

    _____

    Adam's plant

2. What is Elana's plant length?

    _____

    Elana's plant

3. Make a line plot with the students' data.

Looking at the line plot you created above, answer the following questions:

4. Find three data points that create a combined length of 13 inches.

5. How many more plants are $4\frac{2}{4}$ than $3\frac{3}{4}$?

6. Which plant heights have no data?

7. Which plant lengths have the same amount of plants?

8. What is the difference between the largest and smallest plant lengths?

9. When all the lengths added to a total of more than 50 inches, the class was able to plant the seedlings in the garden. Did the plant lengths add up to be more than 50 inches? Explain how you know.

(Answers are on page 191)

UNDERSTANDING HOW ANGLES ARE MEASURED

4.MD.C.5 Recognize angles as geometric shapes that are formed wherever two rays share a common endpoint, and understand concepts of angle measurement

4.MD.C.5.A An angle is measured with reference to a circle with its center at the common endpoint of the rays, by considering the fraction of the circular arc between the points where the two rays intersect the circle. An angle that turns through 1/360 of a circle is called a "one-degree angle," and can be used to measure angles.

4.MD.C.5.B An angle that turns through *n* one-degree angles is said to have an angle measure of *n* degrees.

Bridget and Lisa were learning about angles using fraction circles and spinners. They knew if they moved the spinner from one point on the outside of the circle, back to the same point, they had rotated the spinner 360 degrees.

They had to figure out what fraction of the circle the spinner moved if it went from one edge of the white section to the opposite edge of the white section

1. What fraction of the spinner is white?

2. How many degrees did the spinner move if it went from one edge of the white section to the opposite edge?

3. Explain your reasoning using words, pictures, or numbers.

Next, using the circle to the right, Bridget and Lisa had to figure out what fraction the spinner moved if it went from one edge of the white section to the opposite edge of the white section.

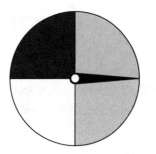

4. What fraction of the spinner is white?

5. How many degrees did the spinner move if it went from one edge of the white section to the opposite edge of the white section?

6. Explain your reasoning using words, pictures, or numbers.

In the spinner to the right, the sections represent thirds. Lisa said the spinner moved 90 degrees from one edge of the green section to the other edge of the green section.

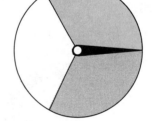

7. Do you agree or disagree with Lisa?

8. Why do you think that? Explain your reasoning with pictures, words, or numbers.

Find the angle measure.

9. If an angle turns through 10 one-degree angles, what is its angle measure?

10. If an angle turns through 133 one-degree angles, what is its angle measure?

(Answers are on page 192)

MEASURING ANGLES

4.MD.C.6 Measure angles in whole-number degrees using a protractor. Sketch angles of specified measure.

Patty and Ashley were exploring angles through a clock activity.
In this activity, using a protractor, they had to find the measures of angles between the hands of a clock.

Using a protractor, explore the following clocks and write the angles they found.

1. Angle measure: _____

3. Angle measure: _____

2. Angle measure: _____

4. Angle measure: _____

5. What do you notice about the angle measures on these two clocks?

1 o'clock   11 o'clock

6. Make a reasonable estimate of what angle measures the two clocks above
    could have. Explain your thinking.

Directions: Draw the hour and minute hand on the clocks to show the following angle
measures:

7. 90 degrees   8. 60 degrees   9. 120 degrees

(Answers are on page 192)

USING ADDITION AND SUBTRACTION TO FIND UNKNOWN ANGLES

4.MD.C.7 Recognize angle measure as additive. When an angle is decomposed into non-overlapping parts, the angle measure of the whole is the sum of the angle measures of the parts. Solve addition and subtraction problems to find unknown angles on a diagram in real-world and mathematical problems (e.g., by using an equation with a symbol for the unknown angle measure).

Directions: Question 1 and 2 are based on the following information.

Julia and Simon were waiting in line to ride the Ferris wheel. They noticed the lever the engineer was using to control the ride had two angles that looked like this:

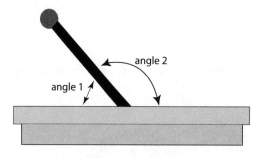

The angles changed as the lever moved forward and backward.

The following table lists three different combinations for angle 1 and angle 2.

Angle 1	Angle 2
30°	150°
80°	100°
120°	60°

1. Using the information in the above table, describe how the angle changed as the lever was pushed forward.

2. What do angles 1 and 2 add up to?

If Julia and Simon only knew one angle, they realized they could figure out the second angle. Help them find the missing angle measure (use the correct notation).

3. Angle 1 = 50°. What does angle 2 measure? _____
    Explain how you figured it out.

4. Angle 2 = 178°. What does angle 1 measure? _____
    Explain how you figured it out.

5. Angle 2 = 2°. What does angle 1 measure? _____
    Explain how you figured it out.

6. What is the measure of the missing angle if ∠CBA = 63°? Explain how you figured it out.

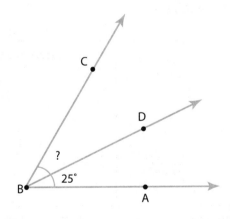

(Answers are on page 192)

IDENTIFYING LINES, ANGLES, AND SHAPES

4.G.A.1 Draw and identify lines and angles, and classify shapes by properties of their lines and angles. Draw points, lines, line segments, rays, angles (right, acute, obtuse), and perpendicular and parallel lines. Identify these in two-dimensional figures.

Directions: Use the following figures to answer Questions 1–3.

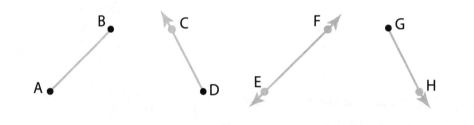

1. Place a circle around the ray.

2. Place a box around the line.

3. Place a star on the line segment.

Directions: Draw the following in each box.

4. Point	6. Two rays that create a right angle
5. Two lines that are perpendicular	7. Two rays that create an obtuse angle

Directions: Identify the type of angles (acute, obtuse, or right) in each figure below.

8. What types of angles do you see?

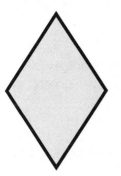

9. What types of angles do you see?

10. What types of angles do you see?

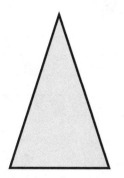

(Answers are on page 193)

CLASSIFYING TWO-DIMENSIONAL SHAPES

4.G.A.2 Classify two-dimensional figures based on the presence or absence of parallel or perpendicular lines, or the presence or absence of angles of a specified size. Recognize right triangles as a category, and identify right triangles.

Directions: Classify the triangles below into two groups. Describe how you are categorizing the triangles at the top of the t-chart (i.e., acute triangles, equilateral triangles).

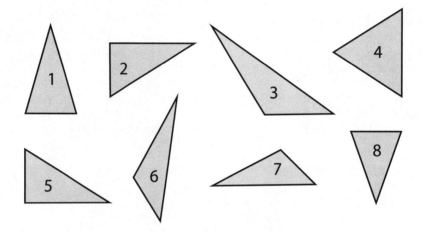

1. Category:	2. Category:

3. Tamara says triangles 2 and 5 are both right triangles. Do you agree or disagree? Explain why or why not.

Directions: Classify the two-dimensional figures below based on the number of parallel sides.

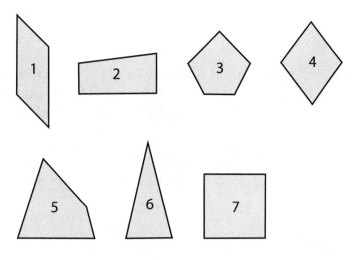

4. More than one pair of parallel lines	5. One pair of parallel sides	6. No pairs of parallel sides

7. Cameron thinks shape 3, above, has more than one pair of parallel sides. Do you think he is correct? Explain why or why not.

8. How could you draw shape 3 so it has exactly one pair of parallel sides?

(Answers are on page 193)

IDENTIFYING LINES OF SYMMETRY

4.G.A.3 Recognize a line of symmetry for a two-dimensional figure as a line across the figure such that the figure can be folded along the line into matching parts. Identify line-symmetric figures, and draw lines of symmetry.

The line of symmetry is a line across the figure so that the figure can be folded along the line into matching parts, such as:

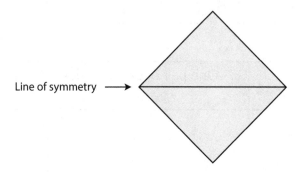

Directions: Determine if the figures below have line(s) of symmetry. If so, draw the line of symmetry.

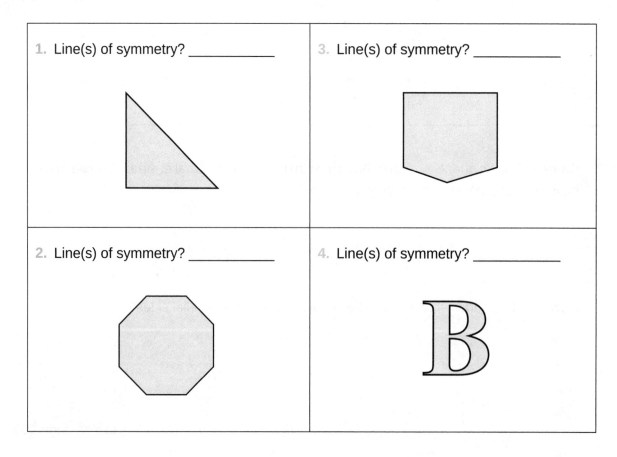

1. Line(s) of symmetry? _____

3. Line(s) of symmetry? _____

2. Line(s) of symmetry? _____

4. Line(s) of symmetry? _____

5. Julian and Ty were finding the lines of symmetry for triangles. They found three lines of symmetry for an equilateral triangle.

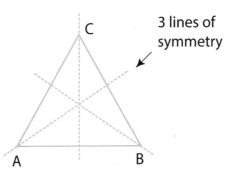

3 lines of symmetry

Ty wondered if the following rule was correct: The number of lines of symmetry equals the number of sides. Julian said that wasn't always the case. Who do you think is correct?

6. Draw a triangle to prove or disprove Ty's theory.

7. Does Ty's rule work with quadrilaterals?

8. Draw a quadrilateral to prove or disprove Ty's theory.

(Answers are on page 194)

MATH
PRACTICE TEST

Directions: Write a matching multiplication equation and comparison statement for questions 1 and 2.

Comparison Statement	Multiplication Equation
1. 42 inches is 7 times longer than 6 inches.	
2.	32 = 8 × 4

3. A large bag of chocolates costs $16. A small bag of chocolates costs $4. How many small bags could Jen buy for the price of a large bag? Write a matching number sentence and show your strategy and solution.

4. Flowers for Mother's Day cost $21. That is 3 times more than the cost of a box of chocolates. How much does the box of chocolates cost? Write a matching number sentence and show your strategy and solution.

Solve the following problems with remainders:

Mom is baking cookies for her Girl Scout troop. She needs 40 cookies.

5. If each box of cookie mix makes 24 cookies, how many boxes would she need?

6. Would she have any cookies left over? If so, how many?

Directions: For questions 7 and 8, find all of the possible whole-number dimensions the rectangles can have. Then determine if the area of each rectangle is prime or composite.

7. Possible factors:
   Is it prime or composite?

   A = 42 sq in

8. Possible factors:

Is it prime or composite?

> A = 27 sq yd

In the following number pattern: 5, 18, 31, 44 …

9. Find the ninth number.

10. Write the rule, and explain how you figured it out.

11. How is the 4 in the number 18,384 different from the 4 in the number 35,419? Explain your reasoning.

12. How is the 3 in the number 18,384 different from the 3 in the number 35,419? Explain your reasoning.

13. Circle the number with the smallest value.

    521,347   541,342   541,140   521,374

14. What is the greatest five-digit number that can be made using these digits with no repetition of digits?

    3   4   7   2   6

    Explain using pictures, words, or numbers why this is the greatest number that can be made.

15. Place 1,802 on the number line below.

1,000   2,000

16. Round 1,802 to the nearest thousands. Explain your reasoning.

17. Tony solved a math problem this way:

$$\begin{array}{r} 458 \\ -\ 256 \\ \hline 112 \end{array}$$

Is his answer correct or incorrect? Use pictures, numbers, and words to show your reasoning.

18. Which number makes this sentence true?

5,904 – _____ = 2, 857

- Ⓐ 3,567
- Ⓑ 2,947
- Ⓒ 3,047
- Ⓓ 3,289

For the end of the year, students in Mrs. Field's class decided to collect pennies to donate to cancer research.

19. If there were 22 students in the class and each student raised 97 pennies, how many pennies did they collect from their class?

20. If 7 classes raised 3,451 pennies each, how much money was raised?

21. Springfield Elementary School held a fundraiser to raise money for a trip to Nature's Classroom where they would learn about science and math in nature. They needed to raise $9,864 for equipment, supplies, and travel expenses. There are 6 grades (Kindergarten–5) in the school. If each grade wanted to contribute an equal amount, how much money does each grade need to raise? Show your strategy using pictures, words, or numbers.

22. How can you use multiplication to prove your solution to question 21 is correct?

23. Order the following fractions from least to greatest:

$$\frac{4}{6}, \frac{1}{2}, \frac{8}{24}$$

24. Find a number between $\frac{2}{3}$ and $\frac{4}{5}$.

25. Jamie, has $\frac{16}{5}$ of her pies left over. After giving some to her friends to take home, she has $\frac{9}{5}$ left. How much pie did she send home with her friends? Use a model to show your thinking.

26. If Jamie started out with 4 full pies, how much pie was eaten at the party?

27. For a class project, each student is given $\frac{3}{4}$ of a yard of ribbon. Suzie, Tina, and Becca decided to combine their ribbons. Which of the following equations could you use to show what they did with numbers?

Ⓐ $\frac{3}{4} \times 3$

Ⓒ $\frac{1}{4} + \frac{1}{4} + \frac{1}{4} + \frac{1}{4} + \frac{1}{4} + \frac{1}{4} + \frac{1}{4} + \frac{1}{4} + \frac{1}{4}$

Ⓔ $3 - \frac{2}{3}$

Ⓑ $\frac{3}{4} + \frac{3}{4} + \frac{3}{4}$

Ⓓ $\frac{3}{4} + 3$

28. Is $\frac{5}{6}$ the same as $5 \times \frac{1}{6}$? Explain why or why not.

29. The shaded area below represents a value less than 1 whole.

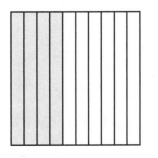

Select all of the values that are equivalent to the white area:

Ⓐ $\frac{4}{10}$

Ⓒ $\frac{6}{10}$

Ⓔ $\frac{3}{5}$

Ⓑ 0.60

Ⓓ 0.06

30. What would the visual model of 0.43 look like on a grid?

31. 48 hundredths = 4 tenths + 8 hundredths

    Is this equation true?

Directions: For questions 32–33, compare the decimals and explain your reasoning:

Fill in the blank using the symbol >, <, or =	Explain your thinking using words and a visual model
32. 7.2 _____ 7.20	
33. 66.3 _____ 66.43	
34. 0.4 _____ 0.07	

35. How many quarts are in 2 gallons?

36. How much does a bag of apples weigh in ounces if it weighs $3\frac{1}{2}$ pounds?

37. Jamie, Jess, and Jill are working together to record a video. Jill's recording is 180 seconds long. Jamie and Jess worked together to record a part of the video that is $3\frac{1}{2}$ minutes long.

    If they put the two recordings together to make one combined video, how many minutes long will it be?

8. Using the information in question 37, if Jamie, Jess, and Jill record a new video that is 10 minutes long, how much longer did they take to record the second video than the first video?

9. Find the width of a rectangular room if the area is 45 feet square and its length is 9 feet.

0. What are two possible areas that a rectangular table can be if the perimeter is 22 inches?

irections: Answer questions 41 and 42 based on the line plot below.

Weight of Hummingbirds in ounces

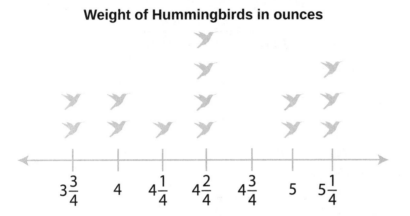

1. What is the difference in weight of the most number of hummingbirds and fewest hummingbirds?

2. Which hummingbird weight(s) has the same number of hummingbirds?

3. If an angle turns through 43 one-degree angles, what is its angle measure?

4. What angle measure does the following clock have?

45. Draw the hour and minute hand on the clock to show the following angle measure: 45 degrees

46. There is a relationship between angle 1 and angle 2.

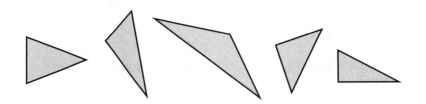

What is the measure of angle 1 if the measure of angle 2 is 145 degrees?

47. What types of angles do you see?

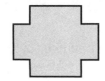

48. Circle the right triangles:

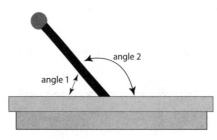

Directions: For questions 49 and 50, determine if the figures have a line(s) of symmetry. If so, draw the line(s) of symmetry.

49.

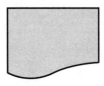

50.

(Answers are on pages 195–198

MATH ANSWERS EXPLAINED

OPERATIONS AND ALGEBRAIC THINKING

Understanding Multiplication
(4.OA.A.1), pages 98–101

1. $8 = 4 \times 2$. The "is" signifies the equal sign (=) and "times" signifies the multiplication symbol (×) to get the equation $8 = 4 \times 2$.

2. $40 = 5 \times 8$. In this problem, "is" signifies the equal sign (=).

3. Many possibilities (e.g., 24 lollipops is 3 times as many as 8 lollipops)

4. $42 = 6 \times 7$. The "is" signifies the equal sign (=) and "times" signifies the multiplication symbol (x) to get the equation.

5. $108 = 12 \times 9$

6. Many possibilities (e.g., 36 apples is 9 times as many as 4 apples)

7. $42 = 6 \times 7$. The "is" signifies the equal sign (=) and "times" signifies the multiplication symbol (×) to get the equation.

8. $28 = 7 \times 4$

9. **Ben's friend has 18 puppies.** $6 \times 3 = 18$ puppies since six three times, or $6 + 6 + 6$, is 18.

10. **I have 18 cats.** If Pali has 9 cats, and we want to have twice the amount, we can say $9 + 9$ or 9×2 is 18.

11. Solution: Sonali's friends will bring 24 stuffed animals.

    $8 \times 3 = 24$

    Equation: $8 \times 3 = ?$ or $8 \times 3 = 24$

Friends:	☺ ☺ ☺ ☺ ☺ ☺ ☺ ☺
Stuffed animals:	‖‖ ‖‖ ‖‖ ‖‖ ‖‖ ‖‖ ‖‖ ‖‖

12. **(C)** Choice C is correct because 12 is the product. "Is" signifies the equal sign and "3 times as many as 4" matches 3×4.

13. **(C)** Choice C is correct because comparing it with A, we know 8×7 is greater than 7×7. The product of 8×7 is 56. In choice B, $6 \times 9 = 54$ and in choice D $11 \times 5 = 55$, which are both close to 56, but still less.

14. **turtles.** To solve this, look for the product of 3×6 muskrats which equals 18. There are 18 turtles.

    $3 \times 6 = 18$

15. **Twice** or **Two times.** If we compared the number of water snakes (14) and herons (7), the relationship between the two numbers is $7 \times 2 = 14$.

    $2 \times 7 = 14$

16. **2; muskrats.** For this problem it is important to look for the relationship between the number of thrushes and all the other animals. There are several possible relationships, but only one that is half the number of thrushes.

    $2 \times 6 = 12$

17. **bullfrogs.** Quadruple means 4 times, and the number of bullfrogs is 4 times the number of muskrats.

    $4 \times 6 = 24$

1. **108 legs.** Double the number of turkeys to get the number of total legs.

2. **30 seeds.** To determine the number of seeds from each pumpkin, take the total number of seeds and divide them by the number of pumpkins. One strategy is to decompose 240 into 24×10. Then, divide 24 by 8 to get 3. If we plug the 3 back into the decomposed number (3×10), the solution is 30 seeds.

3. **$12 in 1 month; $108 in 9 months.** To figure out how much he makes in one month, divide the total from three months by 3 ($36 ÷ 3 = $12). To figure out how much he makes in 9 months, multiply how much he makes in one month by 9 ($12 × 9 = $108).

4. **60 bales of hay.** To figure out how many bales of hay were harvested per day, divide the total number harvested in three days by 3 (180 ÷ 3 = 60).

5. **$3 × 6 = $18.** The apple pie costs $18.

6. **$15 ÷ 3 = $5.** It costs $5 to get into the petting zoo.

7. **$18 ÷ $6 = 3.** He could buy 3 small bags for the price of 1 big bag.

   Solutions for Questions 8 through 12.

Grower	Type of Pumpkin	Circumference of Pumpkin
Demetri	Big Max	8. 30 inches
Sean	Charisma	9. 10 inches
Evan	Iron Man	10. 24 inches
Brandon	Big Rock	11. 34 inches
Soto	Aladdin	12. 12 inches

13. Clue 6 states that Aladdin measures 12 inches around the widest part, which is the circumference of the pumpkin.

14. Clue 4 states that Charisma measures 2 inches less than Aladdin. So if Aladdin's circumference is 12 inches, 12 − 2 = 10. So Charisma's measurement is 10 inches.

15. To figure out the size of Iron Man, you have to use Clue 6, which states the circumference of Aladdin is 12 inches. With that information, we figured out that Iron Man measured 2 times as much as Aladdin. So, Iron Man is 12 × 2 = 24.

16. To figure out the size of Big Max, you have to use Clue 6, which states the circumference of Aladdin is 12 inches. With that information, we need the circumference of Charisma. Clue 4 states that Charisma measures 2 inches less than Aladdin. So if Aladdin's circumference is 12 inches, Charisma's measurement is 10 inches, 12 − 2 = 10. Then, using Charisma's circumference of 10 and Clue 3, which states Demetri's pumpkin measures 3 times Charisma, Big Max's circumference is 30 inches, 10 × 3 = 30.

17. To find Big Rock, you have to use Clue 2, which states "Big Rock measures 4 inches more than Big Max." So using the circumference of Big Max, which is 30 inches, 30 + 4 = 34 inches.

18. Ainsley and Kaya are harvesting pumpkins and squash. They notice the pumpkin vines are 3 times as long as the squash vines. Place a check mark (✔) next to the pair of widths that describe the sizes of the vines.

☐ Pumpkin vine: 8 in
Squash vine: 24 in

☐ Pumpkin vine: 42 in
Squash vine: 36 in

☐ Pumpkin vine: 16 in
Squash vine: 4 in

☐ Pumpkin vine: 20 in
Squash vine: 5 in

✔ Pumpkin vine: 27 in
Squash vine: 9 in

☐ Pumpkin vine: 36 in
Squash vine: 32 in

✔ Pumpkin vine: 15 in
Squash vine: 5 in

☐ Pumpkin vine: 12 in
Squash vine: 3 in

✔ Pumpkin vine: 36 in
Squash vine: 12 in

The three solutions all have a relationship of the pumpkin vine being 3 times longer than the squash vine.

19. They could have 63 squash or more. 9 pumpkins × 7 = 63 squash

20. Part A. The representation is reversed, and the amounts are inaccurate. Instead of showing the model with Kaya having the whole bar, it should represent Demetri's earnings. The bar cut into 3 parts should represent Kaya's earnings with $150 in each part.

Part B. Demetri earned $450. A correct bar model is shown below:

Demetri	$450		
Kaya	$150	$150	$150

Solving Multi-Step Word Problems
(4.OA.A.3), pages 106–107

1. 4 tickets. In 2011 tickets costs $8.50. To find out how many tickets Kaya can buy, divide the total amount of money she has for tickets by the cost of the tickets. $34 ÷ $8.50/ ticket = 4 tickets

2. 3 tickets. In 2012 tickets costs $9.00. To find out how many tickets Kaya can buy, divide the total amount of money she has for tickets by the cost of the tickets. $34 ÷ $9 = 3.7. Since you cannot buy a partial ticket, 3.7 should be rounded down to 3.

3. $36. Kaya needs to purchase 4 tickets. In 2012, tickets cost $9.00. To find the cost of 4 tickets, multiply the cost of the tickets by the number of tickets needed. $9 × 4 people = $36

4. $1.50. To find the difference in the cost of tickets from 2014 and 2011, subtract the cost of the tickets in 2011 form the cost of the tickets in 2014. $10.00 – $8.50 = $1.50

5. She spent 12 weeks saving. 9 × n weeks = $102. If she only saved for 11 weeks, she would only have $99. If she saved for 12 weeks she would have $108, which is enough to pay for the jeans.

6. 7 goodie bags. To get this answer, divide the total number of chocolates by the number of chocolates going into each bag. 30 ÷ 4 = 7.5. She has enough to fill 7 bags with two left over.

7. 6 pairs. She can buy 6 pairs of earrings since $6 × 6 = 36. Seven pairs would cost $42, which is more than she has.

1. Factors: 1×12, 2×6, 3×4
   Prime or Composite: composite

2. Factors: 1×7
   Prime or Composite: prime

3. Factors: 1×29
   Prime or Composite: prime

4. The smallest amount that each could have sold is 24 cookies.

5. 24 cookies, 48 cookies, 72 cookies

6. I chose those three possible amounts because each of them sold cookies in packages of 6 or 8, so the possible amounts must be multiples of both numbers. 24, 48, and 72 are multiples of 6 and 8.

7. Jordyn's age is 3. One way to think about it is if 21 is a multiple of Jordyn's age, then she is either 3 or 7. Since 7 is not a factor of 36, Jordyn must be 3 years old.

8. Dani's age is 18. If the sum of their ages is 21, you can subtract 3 to get Dani's age of 18 years. To check this, 18 is a factor of 36, so it confirms the solution.

Identifying Patterns (4.OA.C.5), pages 110–111

1. Pentagon. The pattern begins with a triangle, then 2 smiley faces, and ends with a pentagon.

2. By continuing the pattern:

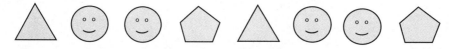

3. Add 5. The difference between each term is 5 ($7 - 2 = 5$, $12 - 7 = 5$, and so on). The 10th number is 47.

4.

	Step 1	Step 2	Step 3	Step 4	Step 5	Step 6
# of pieces	1 square	4 squares	9 squares	16 squares	25 squares	36 squares

5. The rule is to multiply the number of squares in the first row by itself.
   So, 1×1, 2×2, 3×3, 4×4, 5×5, 6×6

6. Many possible solutions. (e.g., 2, 5, 11, 23, and so on)

7. Many possible solutions. (e.g., ▯, ▯▯▯, ▯▯▯▯)

NUMBERS AND OPERATIONS IN BASE 10

Place Value and Division (4.NBT.A.1), pages 112–113

1. 10. Both numbers can be decomposed and recomposed to make an easier problem like
   $(8 \times 100) \div (8 \times 10) \rightarrow (8 \div 8) \times (100 \div 10)$ so the solution is 1×10 or 10.

2. 30. Because $300 \div 10 = 30$

3. The two digits are the same (8s), but their values are different. The value of the 8 in 2,386 is 80 and the value of the 8 in 2,836 is 800.

4. The 3 in David's card is 10 times greater. The numbers can be decomposed by place value to show:

56,739 = 50,000 + 6,000 + 700 + 30 + 9

29,310 = 20,000 + 9,000 + 300 + 10

The value of the 3 in David's card is 300 and the value in Neil's card is 30 (30 × 10 = 300).

5. Possible answers are 74,152; 72,256; and 72,236. In all the numbers, the 7 is worth 70,000. This is 10 times the 7 in 47,312 where the 7 is worth 7,000 (7,000 × 10 = 70,000).

6. (B) This statement is true because the 8 in Neil's number is worth 800, and in David's number it is worth 80. 800 is 10 times the value of 80.

Working with Multi-Digit Numbers (4.NBT.A.2), pages 114–115

1. 523,789. When writing a number, the comma goes after the thousands place value.

2. 749,258. The last two numbers are highest because they begin with 794. The second number is higher because it has 528 instead 258. The first number has the smallest value.

3. 532,935. The second number is the lowest because it is the only number that has a 3 in the hundred-thousands place. The first number is the second lowest because, even though it has a 5 in the hundred-thousands place as the other three do, it only has a 2 in the ten-thousands place. The third number is still less than the last number because it has a 3 in the hundreds place. The last number is the largest because it has a 9 in the hundreds place.

4. (B) 629,273; 623,485; 621,485

5. A. 493,485 < 593,585

   B. 57,250 > 53,285

   C. 256,352 > 25,253

   D. 83,252 < 83,323

6. 85,431. If the largest digit is placed in the largest place value, and all of the numbers are placed in decreasing order as the place value becomes smaller, then the largest possible number is created. With the numbers given, 8 is the largest number, and there are five place values, so the largest number would have 8 in the ten-thousands place value. The next largest number is 5, so it would be in the next largest place value (one-thousands) and so on with 1 being the smallest number.

7. Possible answers are:

   A. 25,295 < 25,385

   B. 58,395 > 43,634

   C. 305,294 < 305,354

   D. 973,536 > 923,194

8. The statement 47,249 > 47,429 is false. If we place the two numbers on a number line, then it is clear that 47,429 is actually greater than 47,249.

9. Pali read more. We could see it clearly by writing both numbers in expanded form and comparing the value of the number in the hundreds place:

Nali = 4,367 = 4,000 + 300 + 60 + 7

Pali = 4,637 = 4,000 + 600 + 30 + 7

10. 600,000 + 20,000 + 9,000 + 300 + 80 + 5

1. Place 1,739 on the number line below.

2. **2,000.** When 1,739 is placed on the number line between 1,000 and 2,000, it is a little less than 1,750 and close to 2,000.

3. **Yes.** It depends on which place value each of them is rounding to. If all three numbers are rounded to the nearest 100,000, then all of the answers would be the same: 100,000. If they were rounded to the nearest 1,000, then the answers would be different.

4. Multiple solutions. It could be 791 rounded to the nearest tens.

   Multiple solutions. It could be 799 rounded to the nearest ones.

   Multiple solutions. It could be 759 rounded to the nearest hundreds.

5. Multiple solutions. It could be 67 + 81. 67 rounded to the nearest tens is 70, and 81 rounded to the nearest tens is 80. If you add these two numbers together, you get 150 (70 + 80 = 150).

Adding and Subtracting Multi-Digit Numbers (4.NBT.B.4), pages 118–119

1. **1,699.** If the numbers were lined up and subtracted using the standard algorithm and regrouping the solution would be a result of:

$$\begin{array}{r} {}^5\!6\,{}^{11}\!2\,{}^{18}\!9\,{}^{15}\!5 \\ -\;4\;\;5\;\;9\;\;6 \\ \hline 1\;\;6\;\;9\;\;9 \end{array}$$

2. **Incorrect.** If you decompose the second number and subtract it from the first number, you have

   492 − 200 = 292
   292 − 50 = 242
   242 − 6 = 236

3. **(B)** If the numbers were lined up and subtracted using the standard algorithm and regrouping the solution would be a result of:

$$\begin{array}{r} {}^5\!6\,{}^{13}\!4\,{}^9\!0\,{}^{14}\!4 \\ -\;2\;\;9\;\;4\;\;7 \\ \hline 3\;\;4\;\;5\;\;7 \end{array}$$

4. The difference in weight between the camel and the bear is 955 pounds.

$$\begin{array}{r} {}^0\!1\,{}^{18}\!8\;\;8\;\;5 \\ -\;\;\;9\;\;3\;\;0 \\ \hline 9\;\;5\;\;5 \end{array}$$

5. The camel weighs 691 more pounds than the buffalo.

$$\begin{array}{r} 1\;{}^7\!8\,{}^{18}\!8\;\;5 \\ -\;1\;\;1\;\;9\;\;4 \\ \hline 6\;\;9\;\;1 \end{array}$$

6. **(B)** The elephant has a weight of 2,707 and the buffalo has a weight of 1,194. If these two numbers are subtracted, the difference is 1,513. This is the only difference that is closest to 1,500.

7. 1,633. If the numbers were lined up and subtracted using the standard algorithm and regrouping the solution would be a result of:

$$\begin{array}{r} {}^3\!4\,^{13}\!3\ \ 8\ \ 7 \\ -\ 2\ \ 7\ \ 5\ \ 4 \\ \hline 1\ \ 6\ \ 3\ \ 3 \end{array}$$

8. 4,587 − 2,954 = 1,633

   If you add 200 to one number, then you must add 200 to the other number to keep the distance the same. So, if you add 200 to 4,387 and 200 to 2,754, the difference would be 1,633.

$$\begin{array}{r} {}^3\!4\,^{15}\!5\ \ 8\ \ 7 \\ -\ 2\ \ 9\ \ 5\ \ 4 \\ \hline 1\ \ 6\ \ 3\ \ 3 \end{array}$$

Multiplying Four-Digit Whole Numbers (4.NBT.B.5), pages 120–121

1. 1,230 × $4 = ?

   ? = $4,920. The two known amounts are the factors and the solution is the product.

   Many possible strategies. Example: partial product

   First, decompose 1,230 = 1,000 + 200 + 30, and then multiply each by $4. So, 1,000 × 4 = 4,000, 200 × 4 = 800, 30 × 4 = 120. To get the solution, add 4,000 + 800 + 120 to get 4,920.

2. The band needs 123 rows. 10 × ? = 1,230, so if we use a rectangular array and decompose the total by 10s, the solution is 123.

10 × 100 = 1,000	10 × 20 = 200	10 × 3 = 30

Total = 1,230

3. Yes. The area model below shows that 20 × 61 = 1,220 with 10 left over is the closest we can get if we put the seats in rows of 20 seats.

20 × 50 = 1,000	20 × 10 = 200	20 × 1 = 20

4. 504 cookies. The equation is 14 × 3 dozen = 14 × 36, since each dozen has 12 cookies and 12 × 3 = 36. So, 14 × 36 = 504.

		36	
		30	6
14	10	10 × 30 = 300	10 × 6 = 60
	4	4 × 30 = 120	4 × 6 = 24

300 + 120 + 60 + 24 = 504 cookies

5. 252 cookies.

		18	
		10	8
14	10	$10 \times 10 = 100$	$10 \times 8 = 80$
	4	$4 \times 10 = 40$	$4 \times 8 = 32$

$100 + 40 + 80 + 32 = 252$ cookies

6. Doubling and halving: double 14 and halve 18 to get 28×9, then $20 \times 9 = 180$ plus $8 \times 9 = 72$.
$180 + 72 = 252$

Dividing Four-Digit Whole Numbers (4.NBT.B.6), pages 122–123

1. Each grade needs to raise $624.

   One strategy is to repeatedly subtract from $3,744.

   $$
   \begin{array}{r}
   3744 \\
   -\ 3600 \quad (6 \times \mathbf{600}) \\
   \hline
   144 \\
   -\ 120 \quad (6 \times \mathbf{20}) \\
   \hline
   24 \\
   -\ 24 \quad (6 \times \mathbf{4}) \\
   \hline
   0
   \end{array}
   $$

   $600 + 20 + 4 = \$624$

2. To prove the solution is correct, place the solution in the number sentence:

   $6 \times ? = \$3,744$

   If we multiply 6×624, we get $3,744.

3. They need to sell 312 cookies. ($624 \div 2 = 312$ cookies) Many possible strategies. One is partial quotients: Decompose 624 to $600 + 20 + 4$, and then divide each part by 2.

   $600 \div 2 = 300$
   $20 \div 2 = 10$
   $4 \div 2 = 2.$

   $300 + 10 + 2 = 312$ cookies.

4. They need to sell 416 tickets. They need to raise a total of $1,248 ($624 + $624 = $1,248).
   $\$1,248 \div 3 = 416$ tickets.

5. They both washed and waxed 150 cars.
   $1,200 divided by $8 = 150$ cars both washed and waxed

6. They washed 160 cars.
   $800 divided by $5 = 160$ cars washed

7. Many possible solutions.

   If we have 102 eggs, and we want to store them in half-dozen egg containers, how many egg containers will we need?

   We need 17 egg containers. Since a dozen equals 12, a half dozen is 6. To figure out how many egg containers would be needed for 102 eggs, you divide 102 by 6 and you get 17.

NUMBERS AND OPERATIONS—FRACTIONS

1. $\frac{3}{4}$ 3 tiles are shaded, and there are 4 total tiles. The fraction of the shaded tiles is $\frac{3}{4}$.

2. $\frac{9}{12}$ 9 tiles are shaded and there are a total of 12 tiles. The fraction of the shaded tiles is $\frac{9}{12}$.

3. **Evan is correct.**

   Another way to think about it is to visually group Molly's parts into 4 groups to see that 3 out of the 4 parts are shaded.

   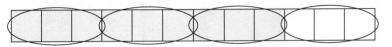

4. Evan needs to fill 4 cups with chocolate chip batter to show $\frac{2}{3}$. Evan's tray is $\frac{4}{6}$ or $\frac{2}{3}$ filled with chocolate chip batter. Grouping them shows how it is equivalent to $\frac{2}{3}$.

   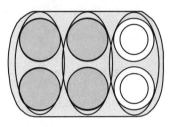

5. Molly needs to fill 8 cups with chocolate chip batter to show $\frac{2}{3}$. Molly's tray is $\frac{8}{12}$ or $\frac{2}{3}$ filled with chocolate chip batter. Grouping them shows how it is equivalent to $\frac{2}{3}$.

   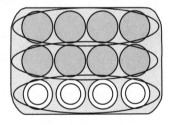

6. Both Evan's and Molly's fractions are equal to $\frac{2}{3}$ because Evan's 6-cup tray can be grouped into 3 parts with 2 cupcakes in each part, and Molly's 12-cup tray can be grouped into 3 parts with 4 cupcakes in each part. For both trays, 2 out of a total of 3 parts are filled with chocolate chip batter. Another way to think about it is with numbers:

   $\frac{4 \div 2}{6 \div 2} = \frac{2}{3}$ and $\frac{8 \div 4}{12 \div 4} = \frac{2}{3}$, so both trays are equivalent to $\frac{2}{3}$.

7. Evan's board can be cut into 5 equal parts by making 4 cuts like this:

   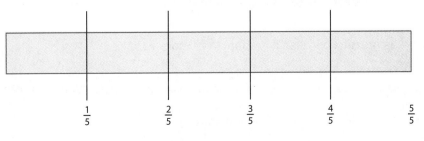

8. Molly's board can be cut into 10 equal parts by making 9 cuts like this:

$\frac{1}{10}$ $\frac{2}{10}$ $\frac{3}{10}$ $\frac{4}{10}$ $\frac{5}{10}$ $\frac{6}{10}$ $\frac{7}{10}$ $\frac{8}{10}$ $\frac{9}{10}$ $\frac{10}{10}$

9. Evan has fewer boards than Molly, but each of Evan's boards is longer than Molly's. There are 5 equivalent fractions: $\frac{1}{5} = \frac{2}{10}$, $\frac{2}{5} = \frac{4}{10}$, $\frac{3}{5} = \frac{6}{10}$, $\frac{4}{5} = \frac{8}{10}$, and $\frac{5}{5} = \frac{10}{10} = 1$ whole. If Evan's and Molly's boards are the same length, then the places where the cuts line up show where the fractions are equivalent.

Comparing Fractions (4.NF.A.2), pages 126–127

1. $\frac{1}{2} < \frac{7}{12} < \frac{5}{6}$. One strategy to use when comparing fractions is to see which benchmarks each fraction is closest to. $\frac{5}{6}$ is close to 1 and $\frac{7}{12}$ is a little more than $\frac{1}{2}$ (because $\frac{1}{2} = \frac{6}{12}$). So in this case $\frac{1}{2}$ has the least value and $\frac{5}{6}$ the greatest.

2. $\frac{2}{8} < \frac{6}{16} < \frac{11}{4}$. In this question, the greatest fraction will be $\frac{11}{4}$, since it is greater than 1 whole. One strategy is to use the relationship of the dominators $\frac{1}{8}$ and $\frac{1}{16}$ to compare $\frac{2}{8}$ and $\frac{6}{16}$. It takes 2 ($\frac{1}{16}$s) to make one $\frac{1}{8}$. So $\frac{6}{16} = \frac{3}{8}$. $\frac{3}{8}$ is greater than $\frac{2}{8}$.

3. $\frac{8}{9} < 1\frac{1}{10} < \frac{9}{5}$. In this question, $\frac{8}{9}$ is the least because there is no whole. $\frac{9}{5}$ is greater than $1\frac{1}{10}$ because it can be converted to $1\frac{4}{5}$, and $\frac{4}{5}$ is greater than $\frac{1}{10}$.

4. $\frac{5}{12} < \frac{5}{6} < \frac{11}{3}$. Using benchmark fractions, $\frac{5}{12}$ is close to $\frac{6}{12}$, which is $\frac{1}{2}$, $\frac{5}{6}$ is close to 1 whole, and $\frac{11}{3}$ is more than a whole.

5. Multiple correct answers. Anything that is greater than $\frac{5}{6}$ but less than $\frac{11}{3}$ would be correct. Examples could be 1 whole, $\frac{14}{6}$, and $3\frac{1}{3}$. There are many possible ways to show this. The two fractions can be drawn out visually or shown on a number line.

6. The true inequalities are circled below:

$\frac{2}{3} < \frac{3}{4}$	$\frac{4}{10} > \frac{5}{8}$	$\frac{6}{8} < \frac{3}{8}$
$2\frac{3}{8} > 2\frac{4}{6}$	$\frac{4}{5} < \frac{1}{3}$	$\frac{7}{3} > \frac{4}{3}$

7. $\frac{7}{10}$ and $\frac{10}{7}$. $\frac{10}{7}$ is greatest because it is greater than a whole.

8. $\frac{6}{12}$ and $\frac{12}{6}$. $\frac{12}{6}$ is greatest because it is equal to 2 wholes.

9. $\frac{10}{7} < \frac{12}{6}$. One strategy is to think of $\frac{12}{6} = 2$ wholes. In order for $\frac{10}{7}$ to equal 2 wholes, the numerator would have to be 14. Since it is not, $\frac{10}{7}$ is less than $\frac{12}{6}$.

1. (C, D)

   (A) $\frac{1}{12} + \frac{1}{12} + \frac{1}{12} + \frac{1}{12} + \frac{1}{12} = \frac{5}{12}$. $\frac{5}{12}$ does not equal $\frac{7}{12}$.

   (B) $\frac{3}{12} + \frac{5}{12} + \frac{1}{12} = \frac{9}{12}$. $\frac{9}{12}$ does not equal $\frac{7}{12}$.

   (C) $1 - \frac{5}{12} = \frac{12}{12} - \frac{5}{12} = \frac{7}{12}$.

   (D) $\frac{9}{12} - \frac{1}{12} = \frac{8}{12} - \frac{1}{12} = \frac{7}{12}$.

   (E) $1 - \frac{7}{12} = \frac{12}{12} - \frac{7}{12} = \frac{5}{12}$. $\frac{5}{12}$ does not equal $\frac{7}{12}$.

2. $\frac{4}{6} = \frac{2}{6} + \frac{2}{6}$

   $\frac{4}{6}$ can be decomposed into two parts with $\frac{2}{6}$ in each part. Or

   $\frac{4}{6} = \frac{1}{6} + \frac{1}{6} + \frac{1}{6} + \frac{1}{6}$

   $\frac{4}{6}$ can be decomposed into four parts with $\frac{1}{6}$ in each part.

3. This can be solved visually:

   If they start with $3\frac{1}{8}$, then mark how many shaded boxes they had to take away with Xs until

   they were left with $1\frac{3}{8}$. The number of boxes with Xs is how much of the candy bars they gave to their friends

			X	X	X	X	X
X	X	X	X	X	X	X	X
X							

   Jimmy and Kevin gave away $\frac{14}{8}$ or $1\frac{6}{8}$ candy bars to their friends.

4. If they started with 5 candy bars and have $3\frac{1}{8}$ remaining, the equation would be $5 - 3\frac{1}{8} = ?$

   To solve it you can take the 3 wholes away from 5 wholes to have 2 wholes remaining.

   Then if you take $\frac{1}{8}$ from 2 wholes, you have $1\frac{7}{8}$ remaining, which is the solution.

   Using an unmarked number line:

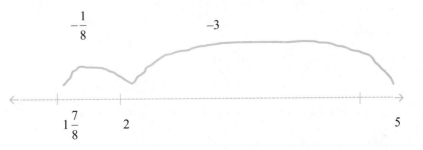

MATH ANSWERS EXPLAINED

5. The second cake has more left because it has $\frac{6}{10} = \frac{3}{5}$ or 0.60 left over. The first cake has only $\frac{1}{2}$ or 0.50.

6. The difference in the amounts left over is $\frac{1}{10}$, since the first cake has $\frac{5}{10}$ left over and the second cake has $\frac{6}{10}$ left over.

7. Max is correct. $\frac{5}{10} + \frac{6}{10} = \frac{11}{10}$ or $1\frac{1}{10}$, which is more than 1 whole.

First cake   Second cake

8. $\frac{1}{6}$ needs to be added to the cup in order to fill it because $\frac{5}{6} + \frac{1}{6}$ = whole.

9. **5 glasses.** If we took one of the glasses that is filled $\frac{5}{6}$ of the way full and gave $\frac{1}{6}$ of it to 5 other glasses, there would be 5 whole glasses—1 empty and 1 filled $\frac{5}{6}$ of the way. See the visual below:

10. $3\frac{1}{6}$ cups more lemonade is needed. We are looking for $5\frac{5}{6} + ? = 9$, so if we add $3\frac{1}{6}$ to $5\frac{5}{6}$ we get 9 whole glasses.

11. $\frac{17}{6} - \frac{9}{6} = \frac{8}{6}$ or $1\frac{2}{6}$ or $1\frac{1}{3}$ of the cakes were sent home with her friends.

12. $\frac{24}{6} - \frac{17}{6} = \frac{7}{6}$ or $1\frac{1}{6}$ of the cakes were eaten.

13. She still needs to send $\frac{3}{6}$ or $\frac{1}{2}$ home with her friends.

14. $\frac{7}{3} + \frac{1}{3} = \frac{8}{3}$ is greater than $\frac{10}{3} - \frac{4}{3} = \frac{6}{3}$

15. $\frac{2}{9} + \frac{1}{9} + \frac{1}{9} = \frac{4}{9}$ is less than $\frac{3}{9} + \frac{2}{9} = \frac{5}{9}$

Multiplying Fractions (4.NF.B.4, 4.NF.B.4.A, 4.NF.B.4.B, 4.NF.B.4.C), pages 132–135

1. $60 \times \frac{3}{4} = 45$ students

15 students	15 students	15 students	

2. Julia's process for solving the problem was correct, but when she took $\frac{1}{4}$ of 60 to get 15, she forgot to multiply it by 3 since she's looking for $3 (\frac{1}{4}s)$.

3. (B, C, D) The following equations describe what they did:

   B. $\dfrac{2}{3} + \dfrac{2}{3} + \dfrac{2}{3} = \dfrac{6}{3} = 2$

   C. $\dfrac{1}{3} + \dfrac{1}{3} + \dfrac{1}{3} + \dfrac{1}{3} + \dfrac{1}{3} + \dfrac{1}{3} = \dfrac{6}{3} = 2$

   D. $\dfrac{2}{3} \times \dfrac{3}{1} = \dfrac{6}{3} = 2$

4. There are 5 chaperones. 45 students ÷ 5 chaperones = 9 students in each group.

5. Agree. Taking 4 $\left(\dfrac{1}{10}s\right)$ is the same as $\dfrac{4}{10}$.

   $\dfrac{1}{10} + \dfrac{1}{10} + \dfrac{1}{10} + \dfrac{1}{10} = \dfrac{4}{10}$. Since multiplication is simply repeated addition, we can take $\dfrac{1}{10}$ and

   add it 4 times to get the same thing as 4 groups of $\dfrac{1}{10}$.

6. 10 people. If 20 people wanted to be Tyrannosaurus rex, then 10 people wanted to be Pterodactyls because that is half of 20 people.

10 people	10 people

   = 20 people

7. 2 people. If you take $\dfrac{1}{5}$ of 10 people, 2 people want to be Demetrodon.

2 people	2 people	2 people	2 people	2 people

   = 10 people

8. 1 person. Half of 2 people is 1 person.

9. Bridget ran 1 lap. Kaya ran 5 laps: 1____2____3____4____5 and we know Bridget ran $\dfrac{1}{5}$ as

   many. If we divide Kaya's 5 laps by 5, then we get 1 lap as the solution.

10. Lucas sprinkles 1 cup onto the brownies and 5 cups onto the lemon cookies. Take the 6 cups and split them into 6 parts:

1 cup on brownies	1 cup on lemon cookies	1 cup on lemon cookies	1 cup on lemon cookies	1 cup on lemon cookies	1 cup on lemon cookies

11. 3 pounds. If there were 4 pounds, then $\dfrac{1}{4}$ pound would be 1 pound. 4 pound $\times \dfrac{1}{4}$ = 1 pound

1 pound	1 pound	1 pound	1 pound

1. $\dfrac{3}{10} + \dfrac{5}{100} = \dfrac{35}{100}$ and $0.3 + 0.05 = 0.35$

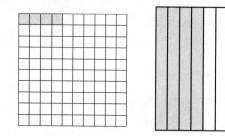

$\dfrac{1}{10} + \dfrac{1}{10} + \dfrac{1}{10} + \dfrac{1}{100} + \dfrac{1}{100} + \dfrac{1}{100} + \dfrac{1}{100} + \dfrac{1}{100} = \dfrac{35}{100}$. Ty has $\dfrac{35}{100}$ or \$0.35 because $\dfrac{3}{10}$ can

be decomposed into three $\dfrac{1}{10}$s, which becomes $\dfrac{30}{100}$s. Combining the $\dfrac{30}{100}$ with $\dfrac{5}{100}$ gives

the solution: $\dfrac{35}{100}$.

2. $\dfrac{6}{10} + \dfrac{2}{100} = \dfrac{62}{100}$ and $0.6 + 0.02 = 0.62$

$\dfrac{1}{10} + \dfrac{1}{10} + \dfrac{1}{10} + \dfrac{1}{10} + \dfrac{1}{10} + \dfrac{1}{10} + \dfrac{1}{100} + \dfrac{1}{100} = \dfrac{62}{100}$

3. **Disagree.** Ty's 20 pennies are only worth 2 dimes. Ty has a total of 3 dimes which is equal to 30 cents, and Terra has 4 dimes which is equal to 40 cents. Terra has more money.

4. **(A, C, D)** The following are equivalent:

   A. $\dfrac{4}{10}$ because 4 parts are shaded out of 10 parts

   C. $\dfrac{40}{100}$ because if we divided the area into 100ths, there would be 4×10 or 40 shaded parts.

   D. 0.40

5. **(B)** 0.04 is not equivalent to the shaded area because the amount of shaded area is not the same.

6. $\dfrac{64}{100}$, 0.64, or $0.6 + 0.04$

7. The mural is 0.77 complete.

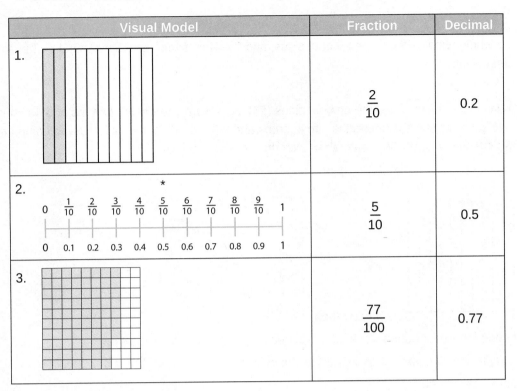

	Visual Model	Fraction	Decimal
1.		$\frac{2}{10}$	0.2
2.		$\frac{5}{10}$	0.5
3.		$\frac{77}{100}$	0.77

4. Therese is correct. $0.40 = \frac{40}{100}$, and if we show it visually, it's the same as $\frac{4}{10}$.

5.

6. 3 hundredths + 5 tenths = .35

   Is this equation true? No

   Explain your reasoning why: If we wrote 3 in the hundredths place value and 5 in the tenths place value, the correct number would be 0.53.

7. $0.40 + 0.3 = \frac{70}{100}$

   Is this equation true? Yes

   Explain your reasoning why: 0.40 + 0.30 = 0.70 and $0.70 = \frac{70}{100}$

8. 27 hundredths = 2 tenths + 7 hundredths

   Is this equation true? Yes

   Explain your reasoning why: 27 hundredths decomposes to make 2 tenths and 7 hundredths.

1. 3.2 = 3.20

    The whole remains the same on both sides, and 2 tenths is the same as 20 hundredths, so they are equivalent.

2. 56.3 < 56.43

    The whole remains the same on both sides (56), so we are comparing 3 tenths and 43 hundredths. If we separate the 43 hundredths into 4 tenths and 3 hundredths, then it is easy to compare 3 tenths and 4 tenths. 4 tenths is greater than 3 tenths, so 56.3 < 56.43.

3. 0.9 > 0.09

    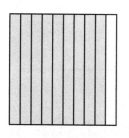 is greater than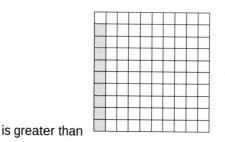

4. It rained the least during week 3. This is because 0.7 in < 1.25 in < 1.4 in.

5. Multiple solutions ranging from 1.26 all the way to 1.49 (i.e., 1.3, 1.39, 1.4, 1.345)

6. Goliath is correct.

    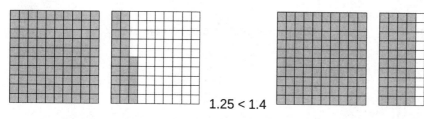 1.25 < 1.4

    Even though 1.25 has more digits, its value is less than 1.4 as shown in the visual.

7. 49.7 < 49.77

    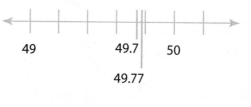

8. 2.8 > 2.08

    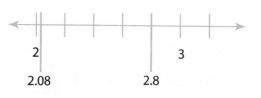

Multiply 12 by the number of feet to get the solution in problems 1 through 6

1. $20 \times 12 = 240$ inches

2. $10 \times 12 = 120$ inches

3. $9 \times 12 = 108$ inches

4. $13 \times 12 = 156$ inches

5. $7 \times 12 = 84$ inches

6. $12 \times 12 = 144$ inches

7. The sharks' length in inches is 12 times the number of feet.

8. Rebecca is correct. 1 yard = 3 feet, so 4 yards = 12 feet.

9. 3 feet (or 36 inches)

10. No, they are not reasonable. 5 centimeters is not equivalent to 500 meters. 500 meters = 50,000 centimeters because 1 meter is equal to 100 centimeters.

11.

Jill	$\frac{1}{2}$ hour	30 minutes
John	3,600 seconds	60 minutes
Jack	40 minutes	40 minutes
Julius	$\frac{3}{5}$ hour	36 minutes
Justin	5,400 seconds	90 minutes

The students from slowest to fastest are: Justin, John, Jack, Julius, Jill. If you convert all the units to minutes, using the information 1 hour = 60 minutes, 1 minute = 60 seconds, then you can compare the length of time it took them to complete the waterslide experiment from slowest to fastest.

In problems 12 through 15, use the relationship of 1 kilogram = 1,000 grams and multiply each kilogram by 1,000 to get the solution:

12. $24 \times 1,000 = 24,000$ grams

13. $9 \times 1,000 = 9,000$ grams

14. $17 \times 1,000 = 17,000$ grams

15. $5 \times 1,000 = 5,000$ grams

In problems 16 through 18, use the relationship of 1 pound = 16 ounces and multiply each pound by 16 to find the solution:

16. $2 \times 16 = 32$ ounces

17. $3 \times 16 = 48$ ounces

18. $4 \times 16 = 64$ ounces

19. **72 ounces.** You know that 1 pound is equal to 16 ounces. So multiple 4 by 16 to find out how many ounces are in 4 pounds: $4 \times 16 = 64$. You still need to convert the addition $\frac{1}{2}$ to ounces, and then add that to 64 to find out the total ounces. Since 1 pound is equal to 16 ounces, then $\frac{1}{2}$ is equal to 8 ounces. $64 + 8 = 72$ ounces.

20. 1 pound = 16 ounces

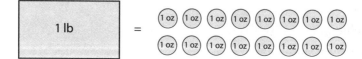

Word Problems Involving Measurements (4.MD.A.2), pages 146–147

1. **$3.90.** Jay has $3.90 because $6 \times \$.25 = \$1.50$ for washing windows, $18 \times \$.05 = \$.90$ for washing dishes, and $15 \times \$.10 = \$1.50$ for drying and putting away dishes. $\$1.50 + \$.90 + \$1.50 = \$3.90$

2. **8 windows.** If he washed, dried, and put away 20 dishes, then he received $3.00 (nickel for washing and dime for drying/putting away $\times$ 20). $5 total – $3 for dishes = $2 for windows. $2 ÷ $.25 = 8 windows.

3. **14.25 feet or $14\frac{1}{4}$ feet.** You know that Sean jumped 10.5 feet and Jackson jumped $3\frac{3}{4}$ feet farther. To find out how many feet Jackson jumped, you add 10.5 feet and $3\frac{3}{4}$ feet. You can either convert 10.5 to a fraction and add it to $3\frac{3}{4}$ or convert $3\frac{3}{4}$ to a decimal and add it to 10.5.

   $$\begin{array}{r} 10.5 \\ +\ 3.75 \\ \hline 14.25 \text{ feet} \end{array}$$
   or $10\frac{1}{2} + 3\frac{3}{4} = 14\frac{1}{4}$ feet

   10.5   14.25

4. **$18\frac{1}{2}$ feet or 18.5 feet.** To find out how far Sean would have to jump to beat Jackson by $4\frac{1}{4}$ feet, you have to add $4\frac{1}{4}$ feet to the distance that Jackson jumped. $4\frac{1}{4} + 14\frac{1}{4} = 18\frac{1}{2}$

5. **8 minutes 20 seconds long.** To find the total number of minutes, you need to add all of the lengths of the songs together. In order to do this, you will need to convert $2\frac{1}{2}$ and 3 minutes to seconds and then add all numbers together and divide by 60 seconds.

   150 seconds + $2\frac{1}{2}$ min (150 sec) + 3 min 20 sec (200 sec) = 500.

   500 seconds ÷ 60 seconds = $8\frac{1}{3}$ min or 8 min and 20 sec.

6. **1 minute 40 seconds.** The question is asking you to find the difference in the length of the set played at the concert and the length of the CD. The set is 10 minutes long, and the CD is 8 minutes and 20 seconds long. Subtract 8 minutes and 20 seconds from 10 minutes to get your answer.

   10 min – 8 min 20 sec = 1 min 40 sec.

7. **$1\frac{1}{2}$ quarts.** If 1 quart is needed for 4 servings, then $1\frac{1}{2}$ quarts is needed for 6 servings.

8. **16 servings.** 1 gallon is equal to 4 quarts. If 1 quart of yogurt makes 4 servings, then 4 quarts would make 16 servings. $4 \times 4 = 16$

Finding Area and Perimeter (4.MD.A.3), pages 148–149

1. **30 feet.** Since the width of section 2 is 3 feet ($3 + 3 + 3 + 3 = 12$) and the width of section 3 is 5 feet ($5 \times 3 = 15$), the length of section 1 is 8 feet ($3 + 5 = 8$). Because the length is 1 foot more than the width, the width is 7 feet. The perimeter is $8 + 8 + 7 + 7 = 30$ feet.

2. **9 square feet.** If the perimeter of the square is 12, then the length of each side is 3 feet (divide 12 by the 4 sides). To find the area, multiply the length of the side by the width:
$3 \times 3 = 9$ square feet.

3. **16 feet.** If section 3 has a length of 3 feet and a width of 5 feet, then $3 + 3 + 5 + 5 = 16$ feet.

4. The perimeter of the 8 feet × 10 feet mural is 36 feet and area is 80 square feet. 8 feet × 10 feet doubled would be 16 feet × 20 feet so the perimeter is $16 + 16 + 20 + 20 = 72$ feet. The area is 320 square feet.

5. **6 feet.** The formula for area is length × width. If they want the area to be 24 feet, and the length is 4 feet, they need to find the number that if multiplied by 4 would equal 24. This number is 6 ($6 \times 4 = 24$)

Line Plots (4.MD.B.4), pages 150–151

1. **5 inches.** Line up the plant to the closest mark on the ruler, which is 5 in.

2. $5\frac{1}{4}$ **inches.** Line up the plant to the closest mark on the ruler, which is $5\frac{1}{4}$ in.

3. To create a line plot, first make a number line with equally spaced numbers. Then place an X above the number on the number line for each data point from the table.

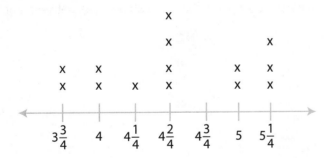

4. $3\frac{3}{4} + 4\frac{1}{4} + 5 = 13$ inches or $3\frac{3}{4} + 4 + 5\frac{1}{4} = 13$ inches.

5. 2 more plants.

6. $4\frac{3}{4}$

7. $3\frac{3}{4}$, 4, 5

8. $1\frac{2}{4}$ inches. $5\frac{1}{4} - 3\frac{3}{4}$

9. Yes, the plant lengths equal $63\frac{2}{4}$ inches. Add up all the lengths to find that they total $63\frac{2}{4}$ inches.

1. $\frac{1}{2}$. If the circle is a whole, half is white.

2. 180 degrees. $(360 \div 2 = 180)$

3. If it is 360 degrees to go all the way around, then half of 360 is 180 degrees.

4. $\frac{1}{4}$. The spinner is broken into 4 parts and one part is white.

5. 90 degrees.

6. If it is 360 degrees around the whole circle, then dividing it by 4 gives us 90 degrees.

7. Disagree

8. $\frac{1}{3}$ of 360 degrees is 120 degrees. It did not move 90 degrees. It moved 120 degrees.

9. The angle measure is 10 degrees, since the sum of each one-degree adds up to 10 degrees.

10. The angle measure is 133 degrees.

1. 90 degrees. A right angle is equal to 90 degrees.

2. 60 degrees. There are 360 degrees around, so if we divide it by 12 parts, there are 30 degrees between each marked number.

3. 180 degrees. If it is a total of 360 degrees around, then half way would be 180 degrees.

4. 120 degrees.

5. The minute hand on both clocks is on 12, but the hour hand is on 1 and 11, both 5 minutes from where the minute hand is.

6. The angle measures are both 30 degrees. As we realized in Question 2, there are 360 degrees around. If we divide the clock by 12 parts, there are 30 degrees between each marked number.

7.   8.   9.

1. As the lever was pulled forward, the degrees for angle 1 increased while the degrees for angle 2 decreased.

2. They add up to 180°.

3. 130°

   $180 - 50 = 130°$ or $50 + ? = 180°$

4. 2°

   $180 - 178 = 2°$

5. 178°

   If the total is 180, subtract 2 degrees to get the solution of 178°

6. 38°

   $63 - 25 = 38°$

1. CD and GH are rays. Rays have only one endpoint.
2. EF is a line. There are no endpoints. It can go on forever in either direction.
3. AB is a line segment. A line segment has two endpoints.
4. Point ●
5.

6.

7.

8. **Acute and obtuse angles.** Two angles are less than 90 degrees and two angles are greater than 90 degrees.
9. **Obtuse angles.** All the angles are equal and greater than 90 degrees.
10. **Acute angles.** All the angles are less than 90 degrees.

Classifying Two-Dimensional Shapes (4.G.A.2), pages 160–161

1. Multiple possible solutions:

    Right triangles – 2, 5
    Acute triangles – 1, 4, 8
    Obtuse triangles – 3, 6, 7

2. Multiple possible solutions:

    Scalene triangles – 2, 3, 5, 6, 7
    Isosceles triangles – 1, 8
    Equilateral triangles – 4

3. **Agree.** They are both right triangles. If a triangle has one 90 degree angle, then it is a right triangle. Triangles 2 and 5 both have 90 degree angles.

4. **1, 4, 7.** All of them have more than one pair of parallel lines. If the top and bottom lines were to be continued, they would never intersect, and if the two side lines were to be continued, they would never intersect.

5. **2.** Only figure 2 has one pair of parallel sides. The top line is slanted, so it is not parallel to the bottom line. If these lines were to be continued, they would intersect.

6. **3, 5, 6.** These figures do not include any parallel lines. All lines would intersect if extended.

7. **Cameron is not correct.** He is not correct because it is a pentagon and none of the sides are parallel. If the sides were extended, they would intersect.

8. If you drew the pentagon to look like a house, it would have one pair of parallel lines. Like this:

Identifying Lines of Symmetry (4.G.A.3), pages 162–163

1. Line(s) of symmetry? _____1_____

2. Line(s) of symmetry? _____8_____

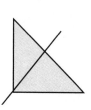

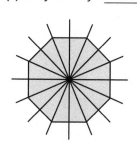

3. Line(s) of symmetry? _____1_____

4. Line(s) of symmetry? _____1_____

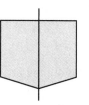

5. **Julian is correct.** It is not always the case. A right triangle with a longer length than width has 3 sides and no lines of symmetry.

6. 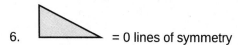 = 0 lines of symmetry

7. **No.** It works only with a square.

8.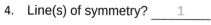

Comparison Statement	Multiplication Equation
1. 42 inches is 7 times longer than 6 inches.	42 = 7 × 6 (4.OA.A.1)
2. Many possible solutions (4.OA.A.1) (e.g., 32 is 8 times greater than 4)	32 = 8 × 4

3. 16 = 4 × ?. The solution is 4, and there are multiple strategies. (4.OA.A.2)

4. $21 = 3 × a; a = 7 (4.OA.A.2)

5. 2 boxes. She needs more than one box because one box will only make 24 cookies. Two boxes would make double that (24 × 2 = 48). (4.OA.A.3)

6. Yes, she would have 8 cookies left over. Since she only needs 40 cookies, and two boxes will make 48 cookies, then 8 cookies will be left over. (48 – 40 = 8 cookies left over) (4.OA.A.3)

7. 42 = 42 × 1, 2 × 21, 3 × 14, 7 × 6. It is composite. (4.OA.B.4)

8. 27 = 3 × 9 and 1 × 27. It is composite. (4.OA.B.4)

9. The ninth number is 109. The numbers are 5, 18, 31, 44, 57, 70, 83, 96, 109. (4.OA.C.5)

10. The rule is +13. If you take the difference between the terms, each difference is 13 units. (4.OA.C.5)

11. In the first number, the 4 is in the ones place value, and in the second number, it is in the hundreds place value. This makes it 100 times greater. (4.NBT.A.1)

12. In the first number, the 3 is in the hundreds place value, and in the second number, it is in the ten thousands place value. This makes it 100 times greater. (4.NBT.A.1)

13. Circle the number with the smallest value.

   (521,347)   541,342   541,140   521,374

   The first and second number have the same numbers in the hundred thousand, ten thousand, and thousand places, but the first number has a lower number in the hundreds place. (4.NBT.A.2)

14. 76,432. Use the greatest number first, then the next greatest number, and so on. (4.NBT.A.2)

15. Place 1,802 on the number line below. (4.NBT.A.3)

   1,000   1,802   2,000

16. 1,802 rounded to the nearest thousands is 2,000. The answer is 2,000 because the number in the hundreds place is 8. This means it has the value of 800, so you only need 200 more to reach 1,000. If you were to round to 1,000, you would be 800 away from that number. 1,802 falls closer to 2,000 than 1,000. (4.NBT.B.3)

17. The solution is incorrect. He subtracted the 4 – 2 and the 5 – 5 incorrectly. The correct solution is 202. (4.NBT.B.4)

   458
   −256
   202

18. **(C)** The correct solution is C because it makes the subtraction sentence true.

$$5\;^{8}9\;^{9}0\;^{14}4$$
$$-\;3\;\;0\;\;4\;\;7$$
$$2\;\;8\;\;5\;\;7$$

Another strategy to find the solution could be to add each answer choice with 2,857 to determine that C is correct. (4.NBT.B.4)

19. **They collected 2,134 pennies.** This question is asking for the total number of pennies collected by the class. Since each student collected the same number of pennies, to find this answer you must multiply the number of students by the number of pennies each collected $22 \times 97 = 2,134$. (4.NBT.B.5)

20. **$241.57 was raised.** This question is asking for the total amount of money raised by 7 classes. This is a two-step problem. The first step is to determine how many pennies were raised in total. If each class raised 3,451 pennies, in order to determine how many were raised in all 7 classes, you need to multiply 3,451 by 7 ($3,451 \times 7 = 24,157$). The next step is to convert the number of pennies to a dollar amount. Since you know that there are 100 pennies in $1, you must divide 24,157 by 100 ($24,157 \div 100 = \$241.57$). (4.NBT.B.5)

21. **Each grade would need to raise $1,644.** The question is asking how much money each grade would need to raise in order to equally contribute to the total money needed. Since you know that the total amount of money needed is $9,864, and there are 6 classes, you can divide 9,864 by 6 to get your answer ($\$9,864 \div 6 = \$1,644$). (4.NBT.B.6)

22. To prove the solution is correct, you would multiply 6 by 1,644. If the answer equals 9,864 then your solution is correct. $6 \times 1,644 = \$9,864$ (4.NBT.B.6)

23. $\dfrac{8}{24}$, $\dfrac{1}{2}$, $\dfrac{4}{6}$. Using benchmark fractions $\dfrac{4}{6}$ is closest to 1 whole, $\dfrac{8}{24}$ is less than half (since half is $\dfrac{12}{24}$). (4.NF.A.2)

24. $\dfrac{11}{15}$ is a number between $\dfrac{2}{3}$ and $\dfrac{4}{5}$ since the value of the denominator is smaller than $\dfrac{1}{3}$ and $\dfrac{1}{5}$.

 Also, $\dfrac{2}{3} = \dfrac{10}{15}$ and $\dfrac{4}{5} = \dfrac{12}{15}$. (4.NF.A.2)

25. $\dfrac{7}{5}$ $\dfrac{16}{5} - \dfrac{9}{5} = \dfrac{7}{5}$ (4.NF.B.3)

26. $\dfrac{4}{5}$ $4 - \dfrac{16}{₹5} = \dfrac{20}{5} - \dfrac{16}{5} = \dfrac{4}{5}$ (4.NF.B.3)

27. **(A, B, C)** (4.NF.B.4)

28. Yes, $\dfrac{5}{6}$ = 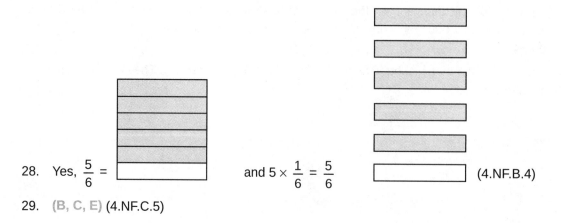 and $5 \times \dfrac{1}{6} = \dfrac{5}{6}$ (4.NF.B.4)

29. **(B, C, E)** (4.NF.C.5)

30.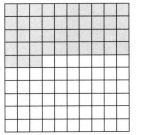

(4.NF.C.6)

31. Yes. (4.NF.C.6)

Fill in the blank using the symbol >, <, or =	Explain your thinking using words and a visual model
32. 7.2 = 7.20	They are both the same because 2 tenths and 20 hundredths are the same (4.NF.C.7)
33. 66.3 < 66.43	3 tenths is less than 4 tenths (4.NF.C.7)
34. 0.4 > 0.07	4 tenths is greater than 0 tenths (4.NF.C.7)

35. 8 quarts. There are 4 quarts in 1 gallon, so if you have 2 gallons you would double that. $4 \times 2 = 8$. (4.MD.A.1)

36. 56 ounces. There are 16 ounces in 1 pound. To convert $3\frac{1}{2}$ pounds to ounces, you would multiply 16 by 3 to get 48. You still need to add the ounces for the remaining $\frac{1}{2}$ pound. You know that 16 ounces is equal to 1 pound, so $\frac{1}{2}$ pound would be half the number of ounces, which is 8. Add 8 and 48 to get your answer of 56 ounces. (4.MD.A.1)

37. $6\frac{1}{2}$ minutes. First you should convert 180 seconds to minutes. You know that 60 seconds is equal to 1 minute, so you would divide 180 by 60: $180 \div 60 = 3$. To find out the total number of minutes, add the 3 minutes to the $3\frac{1}{2}$ minutes for Jamie and Jess's video: $3 + 3\frac{1}{2} = 6\frac{1}{2}$ minutes. (4.MD.A.2)

38. $3\frac{1}{2}$ minutes. This question is asking you to find the difference between the length of the second video and the length of the first video. $10 - 6\frac{1}{2} = 3\frac{1}{2}$ (4.MD.A.2)

39. Width = 5 feet. The formula for finding the area is length × width. You know the length is 9 feet. To find the width, you need to find what number multiplied by 9 equals 45. $9 \times ? = 45$. The answer is 5 ($9 \times 5 = 45$). (4.MD.A.3)

40. 8 length × 3 width or 6 length × 5 width. There are many possible answers. (4.MD.A.3)

41. $\frac{1}{4}$ ounce. The weight of most hummingbirds is $4\frac{2}{4}$ and the weight of the least hummingbirds is $4\frac{3}{4}$. The question is asking you for the difference between the two weights.

$4\frac{3}{4} - 4\frac{2}{4} = \frac{1}{4}$ ounces. (4.MD.B.4)

42. $3\frac{3}{4}$, 4, 5 all have two hummingbirds. (4.MD.B.4)

43. 43° (4.MD.C.5)

44. 120° (4.MD.C.6)

45.

(4.MD.C.6)

46. 35° degrees. (4.MD.C.7)

47. Right angles. (4.G.A.1)

48. Circle the right triangles:

(4.G.A.2)

49. No line of symmetry

(4.G.A.3)

50. 1 line of symmetry through middle.

(4.G.A.3)

APPENDIX A

ENGLISH LANGUAGE ARTS
COMMON CORE STANDARDS

Reading: Literature
Key Ideas and Details
CCSS.ELA-Literacy.RL.4.1   Refer to details and examples in a text when explaining what the text says explicitly and when drawing inferences from the text.
CCSS.ELA-Literacy.RL.4.2   Determine a theme of a story, drama, or poem from details in the text; summarize the text.
CCSS.ELA-Literacy.RL.4.3   Describe in depth a character, setting, or event in a story or drama, drawing on specific details in the text (e.g., a character's thoughts, words, or actions).
Craft and Structure
CCSS.ELA-Literacy.RL.4.4   Determine the meaning of words and phrases as they are used in a text, including those that allude to significant characters found in mythology (e.g., Herculean).
CCSS.ELA-Literacy.RL.4.5   Explain major differences between poems, drama, and prose, and refer to the structural elements of poems (e.g., verse, rhythm, meter) and drama (e.g., casts of characters, settings, descriptions, dialogue, stage directions) when writing or speaking about a text.
CCSS.ELA-Literacy.RL.4.6   Compare and contrast the point of view from which different stories are narrated, including the difference between first- and third-person narrations.
Integration of Knowledge and Ideas
CCSS.ELA-Literacy.RL.4.7   Make connections between the text of a story or drama and a visual or oral presentation of the text, identifying where each version reflects specific descriptions and directions in the text.
CCSS.ELA-Literacy.RL.4.8   (RL.4.8 not applicable to literature)
CCSS.ELA-Literacy.RL.4.9   Compare and contrast the treatment of similar themes and topics (e.g., opposition of good and evil) and patterns of events (e.g., the quest) in stories, myths, and traditional literature from different cultures.
Range of Reading and Level of Text Complexity
CCSS.ELA-Literacy.RL.4.10   By the end of the year, read and comprehend literature, including stories, dramas, and poetry, in the grades 4–5 text complexity band proficiently, with scaffolding as needed at the high end of the range.
Reading: Informational Text
Key Ideas and Details
CCSS.ELA-Literacy.RI.4.1   Refer to details and examples in a text when explaining what the text says explicitly and when drawing inferences from the text.
CCSS.ELA-Literacy.RI.4.2   Determine the main idea of a text and explain how it is supported by key details; summarize the text.
CCSS.ELA-Literacy.RI.4.3   Explain events, procedures, ideas, or concepts in a historical, scientific, or technical text, including what happened and why, based on specific information in the text.

CCSS.ELA-Literacy.RI.4.4 Determine the meaning of general academic and domain-specific words or phrases in a text relevant to a *grade 4 topic or subject area*.

CCSS.ELA-Literacy.RI.4.5 Describe the overall structure (e.g., chronology, comparison, cause/effect, problem/solution) of events, ideas, concepts, or information in a text or part of a text.

CCSS.ELA-Literacy.RI.4.6 Compare and contrast a firsthand and secondhand account of the same event or topic; describe the differences in focus and the information provided.

Integration of Knowledge and Ideas

CCSS.ELA-Literacy.RI.4.7 Interpret information presented visually, orally, or quantitatively (e.g., in charts, graphs, diagrams, time lines, animations, or interactive elements on Web pages) and explain how the information contributes to an understanding of the text in which it appears.

CCSS.ELA-Literacy.RI.4.8 Explain how an author uses reasons and evidence to support particular points in a text.

CCSS.ELA-Literacy.RI.4.9 Integrate information from two texts on the same topic in order to write or speak about the subject knowledgeably.

Range of Reading and Level of Text Complexity

CCSS.ELA-Literacy.RI.4.10 By the end of year, read and comprehend informational texts, including history/social studies, science, and technical texts, in the grades 4–5 text complexity band proficiently, with scaffolding as needed at the high end of the range.

Reading Foundational Skills

Phonics and Word Recognition

CCSS.ELA-Literacy.RF.4.3 Know and apply grade-level phonics and word analysis skills in decoding words.

> **CCSS.ELA-Literacy.RF.4.3.A** Use combined knowledge of all letter-sound correspondences, syllabication patterns, and morphology (e.g., roots and affixes) to read accurately unfamiliar multisyllabic words in context and out of context.

Fluency

CCSS.ELA-Literacy.RF.4.4 Read with sufficient accuracy and fluency to support comprehension.

> **CCSS.ELA-Literacy.RF.4.4.A** Read grade-level text with purpose and understanding.
>
> **CCSS.ELA-Literacy.RF.4.4.B** Read grade-level prose and poetry orally with accuracy, appropriate rate, and expression on successive readings.
>
> **CCSS.ELA-Literacy.RF.4.4.C** Use context to confirm or self-correct word recognition and understanding, rereading as necessary.

Writing

Text Types and Purposes

CCSS.ELA-Literacy.W.4.1 Write opinion pieces on topics or texts, supporting a point of view with reasons and information.

> **CCSS.ELA-Literacy.W.4.1.A** Introduce a topic or text clearly, state an opinion, and create an organizational structure in which related ideas are grouped to support the writer's purpose.
>
> **CCSS.ELA-Literacy.W.4.1.B** Provide reasons that are supported by facts and details.
>
> **CCSS.ELA-Literacy.W.4.1.C** Link opinion and reasons using words and phrases (e.g., *for instance*, *in order to*, *in addition*).
>
> **CCSS.ELA-Literacy.W.4.1.D** Provide a concluding statement or section related to the opinion presented.

CCSS.ELA-Literacy.W.4.2   Write informative/explanatory texts to examine a topic and convey ideas and information clearly.

  CCSS.ELA-Literacy.W.4.2.A   Introduce a topic clearly and group related information in paragraphs and sections; include formatting (e.g., headings), illustrations, and multimedia when useful to aiding comprehension.

  CCSS.ELA-Literacy.W.4.2.B   Develop the topic with facts, definitions, concrete details, quotations, or other information and examples related to the topic.

  CCSS.ELA-Literacy.W.4.2.C   Link ideas within categories of information using words and phrases (e.g., *another*, *for example*, *also*, *because*).

  CCSS.ELA-Literacy.W.4.2.D   Use precise language and domain-specific vocabulary to inform about or explain the topic.

  CCSS.ELA-Literacy.W.4.2.E   Provide a concluding statement or section related to the information or explanation presented.

CCSS.ELA-Literacy.W.4.3   Write narratives to develop real or imagined experiences or events using effective technique, descriptive details, and clear event sequences.

  CCSS.ELA-Literacy.W.4.3.A   Orient the reader by establishing a situation and introducing a narrator and/or characters; organize an event sequence that unfolds naturally.

  CCSS.ELA-Literacy.W.4.3.B   Use dialogue and description to develop experiences and events or show the responses of characters to situations.

  CCSS.ELA-Literacy.W.4.3.C   Use a variety of transitional words and phrases to manage the sequence of events.

  CCSS.ELA-Literacy.W.4.3.D   Use concrete words and phrases and sensory details to convey experiences and events precisely.

  CCSS.ELA-Literacy.W.4.3.E   Provide a conclusion that follows from the narrated experiences or events.

Production and Distribution of Writing

CCSS.ELA-Literacy.W.4.4   Produce clear and coherent writing in which the development and organization are appropriate to task, purpose, and audience. (Grade-specific expectations for writing types are defined in standards 1–3 above.)

CCSS.ELA-Literacy.W.4.5   With guidance and support from peers and adults, develop and strengthen writing as needed by planning, revising, and editing. (Editing for conventions should demonstrate command of Language standards 1–3 up to and including grade 4 here.)

CCSS.ELA-Literacy.W.4.6   With some guidance and support from adults, use technology, including the Internet, to produce and publish writing as well as to interact and collaborate with others; demonstrate sufficient command of keyboarding skills to type a minimum of one page in a single sitting.

Research to Build and Present Knowledge

CCSS.ELA-Literacy.W.4.7   Conduct short research projects that builds knowledge through investigation of different aspects of a topic.

CCSS.ELA-Literacy.W.4.8   Recall relevant information from experiences or gather relevant information from print and digital sources; take notes and categorize information, and provide a list of sources.

CCSS.ELA-Literacy.W.4.9   Draw evidence from literary or informational texts to support analysis, reflection, and research.

  CCSS.ELA-Literacy.W.4.9.A   Apply *grade 4 Reading standards* to literature (e.g., "Describe in depth a character, setting, or event in a story or drama, drawing on specific details in the text [e.g., a character's thoughts, words, or actions]").

  CCSS.ELA-Literacy.W.4.9.B   Apply *grade 4 Reading standard*s to informational texts (e.g., "Explain how an author uses reasons and evidence to support particular points in a text").

Range of Writing

CCSS.ELA-Literacy.W.4.10   Write routinely over extended time frames (time for research, reflection, and revision) and shorter time frames (a single sitting or a day or two) for a range of discipline-specific tasks, purposes, and audiences.

Speaking and Listening

Comprehension and Collaboration

CCSS.ELA-Literacy.SL.4.1   Engage effectively in a range of collaborative discussions (one-on-one, in groups, and teacher-led) with diverse partners on grade 4 topics and texts, building on others' ideas and expressing their own clearly.

   CCSS.ELA-Literacy.SL.4.1.A   Come to discussions prepared, having read or studied required material; explicitly draw on that preparation and other information known about the topic to explore ideas under discussion.

   CCSS.ELA-Literacy.SL.4.1.B   Follow agreed-upon rules for discussions and carry out assigned roles.

   CCSS.ELA-Literacy.SL.4.1.C   Pose and respond to specific questions to clarify or follow up on information, and make comments that contribute to the discussion and link to the remarks of others.

   CCSS.ELA-Literacy.SL.4.1.D   Review the key ideas expressed and explain their own ideas and understanding in light of the discussion.

CCSS.ELA-Literacy.SL.4.2   Paraphrase portions of a text read aloud or information presented in diverse media and formats, including visually, quantitatively, and orally.

CCSS.ELA-Literacy.SL.4.3   Identify the reasons and evidence a speaker provides to support particular points.

Presentation of Knowledge and Ideas

CCSS.ELA-Literacy.SL.4.4   Report on a topic or text, tell a story, or recount an experience in an organized manner, using appropriate facts and relevant, descriptive details to support main ideas or themes; speak clearly at an understandable pace.

CCSS.ELA-Literacy.SL.4.5   Add audio recordings and visual displays to presentations when appropriate to enhance the development of main ideas or themes.

CCSS.ELA-Literacy.SL.4.6   Differentiate between contexts that call for formal English (e.g., presenting ideas) and situations where informal discourse is appropriate (e.g., small-group discussion); use formal English when appropriate to task and situation. (See grade 4 Language standards for specific expectations.)

Language

Conventions of Standard English

CCSS.ELA-Literacy.L.4.1   Demonstrate command of the conventions of standard English grammar and usage when writing or speaking.

   CCSS.ELA-Literacy.L.4.1.A   Use relative pronouns (*who, whose, whom, which, that*) and relative adverbs (*where, when, why*).

   CCSS.ELA-Literacy.L.4.1.B   Form and use the progressive (e.g., *I was walking; I am walking; I will be walking*) verb tenses.

   CCSS.ELA-Literacy.L.4.1.C   Use modal auxiliaries (e.g., *can, may, must*) to convey various conditions.

   CCSS.ELA-Literacy.L.4.1.D   Order adjectives within sentences according to conventional patterns (e.g., *a small red bag* rather than *a red small bag*).

   CCSS.ELA-Literacy.L.4.1.E   Form and use prepositional phrases.

   CCSS.ELA-Literacy.L.4.1.F   Produce complete sentences, recognizing and correcting inappropriate fragments and run-ons.

   CCSS.ELA-Literacy.L.4.1.G   Correctly use frequently confused words (e.g., *to, too, two; there, their*).

CCSS.ELA-Literacy.L.4.2   Demonstrate command of the conventions of standard English capitalization, punctuation, and spelling when writing.

CCSS.ELA-Literacy.L.4.2.A   Use correct capitalization.

CCSS.ELA-Literacy.L.4.2.B   Use commas and quotation marks to mark direct speech and quotations from a text.

CCSS.ELA-Literacy.L.4.2.C   Use a comma before a coordinating conjunction in a compound sentence.

CCSS.ELA-Literacy.L.4.2.D   Spell grade-appropriate words correctly, consulting references as needed.

Knowledge of Language

CCSS.ELA-Literacy.L.4.3   Use knowledge of language and its conventions when writing, speaking, reading, or listening.

CCSS.ELA-Literacy.L.4.3.A   Choose words and phrases to convey ideas precisely.

CCSS.ELA-Literacy.L.4.3.B   Choose punctuation for effect.

CCSS.ELA-Literacy.L.4.3.C   Differentiate between contexts that call for formal English (e.g., presenting ideas) and situations where informal discourse is appropriate (e.g., small-group discussion).

Vocabulary Acquisition and Use

CCSS.ELA-Literacy.L.4.4   Determine or clarify the meaning of unknown and multiple-meaning words and phrases based on grade 4 reading and content, choosing flexibly from a range of strategies.

CCSS.ELA-Literacy.L.4.4.A   Use context (e.g., definitions, examples, or restatements in text) as a clue to the meaning of a word or phrase.

CCSS.ELA-Literacy.L.4.4.B   Use common, grade-appropriate Greek and Latin affixes and roots as clues to the meaning of a word (e.g., *telegraph*, *photograph*, *autograph*).

CCSS.ELA-Literacy.L.4.4.C   Consult reference materials (e.g., dictionaries, glossaries, thesauruses), both print and digital, to find the pronunciation and determine or clarify the precise meaning of key words and phrases.

CCSS.ELA-Literacy.L.4.5   Demonstrate understanding of figurative language, word relationships, and nuances in word meanings.

CCSS.ELA-Literacy.L.4.5.A   Explain the meaning of simple similes and metaphors (e.g., *as pretty as a picture*) in context.

CCSS.ELA-Literacy.L.4.5.B   Recognize and explain the meaning of common idioms, adages, and proverbs.

CCSS.ELA-Literacy.L.4.5.C   Demonstrate understanding of words by relating them to their opposites (antonyms) and to words with similar but not identical meanings (synonyms).

CCSS.ELA-Literacy.L.4.6   Acquire and use accurately grade-appropriate general academic and domain-specific words and phrases, including those that signal precise actions, emotions, or states of being (e.g., quizzed, whined, stammered) and that are basic to a particular topic (e.g., *wildlife*, *conservation*, and *endangered* when discussing animal preservation).

APPENDIX B

MATH COMMON CORE STANDARDS

Operations and Algebraic Thinking
Use the four operations with whole numbers to solve problems
CCSS.Math.Content.4.OA.A.1 Interpret a multiplication equation as a comparison, e.g., interpret $35 = 5 \times 7$ as a statement that 35 is 5 times as many as 7 and 7 times as many as 5. Represent verbal statements of multiplicative comparisons as multiplication equations.
CCSS.Math.Content.4.OA.A.2 Multiply or divide to solve word problems involving multiplicative comparison, e.g., by using drawings and equations with a symbol for the unknown number to represent the problem, distinguishing multiplicative comparison from additive comparison.
CCSS.Math.Content.4.OA.A.3 Solve multistep word problems posed with whole numbers and having whole-number answers using the four operations, including problems in which remainders must be interpreted. Represent these problems using equations with a letter standing for the unknown quantity. Assess the reasonableness of answers using mental computation and estimation strategies including rounding.
Gain familiarity with factors and multiples
CCSS.Math.Content.4.OA.B.4 Find all factor pairs for a whole number in the range 1–100. Recognize that a whole number is a multiple of each of its factors. Determine whether a given whole number in the range 1–100 is a multiple of a given one-digit number. Determine whether a given whole number in the range 1–100 is prime or composite.
Generate and analyze patterns
CCSS.Math.Content.4.OA.C.5 Generate a number or shape pattern that follows a given rule. Identify apparent features of the pattern that were not explicit in the rule itself. *For example, given the rule "Add 3" and the starting number 1, generate terms in the resulting sequence and observe that the terms appear to alternate between odd and even numbers. Explain informally why the numbers will continue to alternate in this way.*
Numbers and Operations in Base 10
Generalize place value understanding for multi-digit whole numbers
CCSS.Math.Content.4.NBT.A.1 Recognize that in a multi-digit whole number, a digit in one place represents ten times what it represents in the place to its right. *For example, recognize that $700 \div 70 = 10$ by applying concepts of place value and division.*
CCSS.Math.Content.4.NBT.A.2 Read and write multi-digit whole numbers using base-ten numerals, number names, and expanded form. Compare two multi-digit numbers based on meanings of the digits in each place, using >, =, and < symbols to record the results of comparisons.
CCSS.Math.Content.4.NBT.A.3 Use place value understanding to round multi-digit whole numbers to any place.
Use place value understanding and properties of operations to perform multi-digit arithmetic
CCSS.Math.Content.4.NBT.B.4 Fluently add and subtract multi-digit whole numbers using the standard algorithm.
CCSS.Math.Content.4.NBT.B.5 Multiply a whole number of up to four digits by a one-digit whole number, and multiply two two-digit numbers, using strategies based on place value and the properties of operations. Illustrate and explain the calculation by using equations, rectangular arrays, and/or area models.

CCSS.Math.Content.4.NBT.B.6 Find whole-number quotients and remainders with up to four-digit dividends and one-digit divisors, using strategies based on place value, the properties of operations, and/or the relationship between multiplication and division. Illustrate and explain the calculation by using equations, rectangular arrays, and/or area models.

Numbers and Operations—Fractions

Extend understanding of fraction equivalence and ordering

CCSS.Math.Content.4.NF.A.1 Explain why a fraction a/b is equivalent to a fraction $(n \times a)/(n \times b)$ by using visual fraction models, with attention to how the number and size of the parts differ even though the two fractions themselves are the same size. Use this principle to recognize and generate equivalent fractions.

CCSS.Math.Content.4.NF.A.2 Compare two fractions with different numerators and different denominators, e.g., by creating common denominators or numerators, or by comparing to a benchmark fraction such as 1/2. Recognize that comparisons are valid only when the two fractions refer to the same whole. Record the results of comparisons with symbols >, =, or <, and justify the conclusions, e.g., by using a visual fraction model.

Build fractions from unit fractions

CCSS.Math.Content.4.NF.B.3 Understand a fraction a/b with $a > 1$ as a sum of fractions $1/b$.

    CCSS.Math.Content.4.NF.B.3.A Understand addition and subtraction of fractions as joining and separating parts referring to the same whole.

    CCSS.Math.Content.4.NF.B.3.B Decompose a fraction into a sum of fractions with the same denominator in more than one way, recording each decomposition by an equation. Justify decompositions, e.g., by using a visual fraction model. *Examples: 3/8 = 1/8 + 1/8 + 1/8 ; 3/8 = 1/8 + 2/8 ; 2 1/8 = 1 + 1 + 1/8 = 8/8 + 8/8 + 1/8.*

    CCSS.Math.Content.4.NF.B.3.C Add and subtract mixed numbers with like denominators, e.g., by replacing each mixed number with an equivalent fraction, and/or by using properties of operations and the relationship between addition and subtraction.

    CCSS.Math.Content.4.NF.B.3.D Solve word problems involving addition and subtraction of fractions referring to the same whole and having like denominators, e.g., by using visual fraction models and equations to represent the problem.

CCSS.Math.Content.4.NF.B.4 Apply and extend previous understandings of multiplication to multiply a fraction by a whole number.

    CCSS.Math.Content.4.NF.B.4.A Understand a fraction a/b as a multiple of $1/b$. *For example, use a visual fraction model to represent 5/4 as the product 5 × (1/4), recording the conclusion by the equation 5/4 = 5 × (1/4).*

    CCSS.Math.Content.4.NF.B.4.B Understand a multiple of a/b as a multiple of $1/b$, and use this understanding to multiply a fraction by a whole number. *For example, use a visual fraction model to express 3 × (2/5) as 6 × (1/5), recognizing this product as 6/5. (In general, n × (a/b) = (n × a)/b.)*

    CCSS.Math.Content.4.NF.B.4.C Solve word problems involving multiplication of a fraction by a whole number, e.g., by using visual fraction models and equations to represent the problem. *For example, if each person at a party will eat 3/8 of a pound of roast beef, and there will be 5 people at the party, how many pounds of roast beef will be needed? Between what two whole numbers does your answer lie?*

Understand decimal notation for fractions, and compare decimal fractions

CCSS.Math.Content.4.NF.C.5 Express a fraction with denominator 10 as an equivalent fraction with denominator 100, and use this technique to add two fractions with respective denominators 10 and 100.[2] *For example, express 3/10 as 30/100, and add 3/10 + 4/100 = 34/100.*

CCSS.Math.Content.4.NF.C.6 Use decimal notation for fractions with denominators 10 or 100. *For example, rewrite 0.62 as 62/100; describe a length as 0.62 meters; locate 0.62 on a number line diagram.*

CCSS.Math.Content.4.NF.C.7 Compare two decimals to hundredths by reasoning about their size. Recognize that comparisons are valid only when the two decimals refer to the same whole. Record the results of comparisons with the symbols >, =, or <, and justify the conclusions, e.g., by using a visual model.

Solve problems involving measurement and conversion of measurements

CCSS.Math.Content.4.MD.A.1   Know relative sizes of measurement units within one system of units including km, m, cm; kg, g; lb, oz.; l, ml; hr, min, sec. Within a single system of measurement, express measurements in a larger unit in terms of a smaller unit. Record measurement equivalents in a two-column table. *For example, know that 1 ft is 12 times as long as 1 in. Express the length of a 4 ft snake as 48 in. Generate a conversion table for feet and inches listing the number pairs (1, 12), (2, 24), (3, 36), ...*

CCSS.Math.Content.4.MD.A.2   Use the four operations to solve word problems involving distances, intervals of time, liquid volumes, masses of objects, and money, including problems involving simple fractions or decimals, and problems that require expressing measurements given in a larger unit in terms of a smaller unit. Represent measurement quantities using diagrams such as number line diagrams that feature a measurement scale.

CCSS.Math.Content.4.MD.A.3   Apply the area and perimeter formulas for rectangles in real world and mathematical problems. *For example, find the width of a rectangular room given the area of the flooring and the length, by viewing the area formula as a multiplication equation with an unknown factor.*

Represent and interpret data

CCSS.Math.Content.4.MD.B.4   Make a line plot to display a data set of measurements in fractions of a unit (1/2, 1/4, 1/8). Solve problems involving addition and subtraction of fractions by using information presented in line plots. *For example, from a line plot find and interpret the difference in length between the longest and shortest specimens in an insect collection.*

Geometric measurement: understand concepts of angle and measure angles

CCSS.Math.Content.4.MD.C.5   Recognize angles as geometric shapes that are formed wherever two rays share a common endpoint, and understand concepts of angle measurement:

CCSS.Math.Content.4.MD.C.5.A   An angle is measured with reference to a circle with its center at the common endpoint of the rays, by considering the fraction of the circular arc between the points where the two rays intersect the circle. An angle that turns through 1/360 of a circle is called a "one-degree angle," and can be used to measure angles.

CCSS.Math.Content.4.MD.C.5.B   An angle that turns through n one-degree angles is said to have an angle measure of n degrees.

CCSS.Math.Content.4.MD.C.6   Measure angles in whole-number degrees using a protractor. Sketch angles of specified measure.

CCSS.Math.Content.4.MD.C.7   Recognize angle measure as additive. When an angle is decomposed into non-overlapping parts, the angle measure of the whole is the sum of the angle measures of the parts. Solve addition and subtraction problems to find unknown angles on a diagram in real world and mathematical problems, e.g., by using an equation with a symbol for the unknown angle measure.

Geometry

Draw and identify lines and angles, and classify shapes by properties of their lines and angles

CCSS.Math.Content.4.G.A.1   Draw points, lines, line segments, rays, angles (right, acute, obtuse), and perpendicular and parallel lines. Identify these in two-dimensional figures.

CCSS.Math.Content.4.G.A.2   Classify two-dimensional figures based on the presence or absence of parallel or perpendicular lines, or the presence or absence of angles of a specified size. Recognize right triangles as a category, and identify right triangles.

CCSS.Math.Content.4.G.A.3   Recognize a line of symmetry for a two-dimensional figure as a line across the figure such that the figure can be folded along the line into matching parts. Identify line-symmetric figures and draw lines of symmetry.